9-89

25¢

The Twelve

The Twelve

by

CARLOS FRANQUI

Translated into English by
ALBERT B. TEICHNER

Introduction by
TANA de GÁMEZ

LYLE STUART INC. • NEW YORK

AN INTRODUCTION

by

Tana de Gámez

In the genre of candidly recorded living history—nonfiction novels, as-told-to books, the more reflective journalistic profile —some worthy examples perform in reverse to the microscope which shows the complex world contained in a speck of seemingly inert matter: they reveal how disarmingly simple can be the components of a formidable universe. The Twelve, as no other book available on the subject, offers that deceivingly small but immensely important window to the Cuban Revolution. Here, for the first time, from the unrehearsed voices of its principals, if not its stars, are the early hopes and agonizing setbacks, the first trials and triumphs of the most original and successful national reformation movement of our days.

Twelve voices speak to us in this book, those of three women and nine men, among them the author's. Actually, one could say that the author in this case is the tape-recorder, for this is not an as-told-to book, nor one of interviews, but rather a collection of talks recorded *en famille* by a distinguished journalist who acts as the infrequent and tactful moderator of reminiscences. The spontaneity which prevails in those conversations is the book's greatest charm. Historically it is its most valuable asset.

The book focuses on the early struggles of the Revolution, on the years of intrigue and danger in the Underground, the days

5

of personal heroism, individual sacrifices and soaring idealism hushed in homes and universities, and in the jails and torture chambers of Havana and Santiago. In ingenuous and often colorful terms the participants evoke and reflect upon the saga of some 250 men and women in their teens and twenties who dared act to rescue their country from a corrupt and ruthless military dictatorship, pitting their Lilliputian strength against Batista's U.S.-advised and equipped Armed Forces and his Gestapo-style police. The book's unassuming tone calls for a brief historical review of some of the events referred to by the participants.

They were students, workers, young professionals, teachers, artists, clerks. Some were poor, a few were rich, most of them were sheltered sons and daughters of middle class families. The majority worked in spartan clandestinity, a few with the knowledge and silent admiration of their trembling parents.

They were led and inspired by an articulate twenty six year old rookie lawyer, himself the son of a wealthy planter and educated in one of Havana's exclusive Roman Catholic schools, the College of the Marian Fathers. His had been the only voice which dared condemn publicly Batista's military coup d'etat of 1952, three months before national elections. In fact, four days after the coup and ten days before the United States officially recognized the dictator, that lone voice went on record at one of Cuba's highest civil courts, indicting the tyrant and asking for a public trial. His name was Fidel Castro y Ruz.

For nearly a year the young rebels trained secretly at the residence of a partisan in the fashionable Vedado district of Havana. It was not far from the local police precinct and only a few blocks from the interrogation cells of the dreaded Service of Military Intelligence. They trained without disrupting their normal activities in and out classes, jobs, homes, restaurants, stores, in the middle of a busy modern city. (Can one imagine such goings on in Park Avenue, Mayfair, or Passy?)

They sold their books and jewelry, they took extra jobs and

mortgaged their cars, properties, businesses, until they raised fifteen thousand dollars with which to purchase guns and uniforms. They had no outside help, no offers of support from powerful individuals, organizations, or foreign land. (Neither did they have to contend, as yet, with the antagonism of the then unsuspecting United States and the long-reaching arm of its CIA and Green Berets.) So meager was their arsenal that when time came for the uprising many anxious and well-trained partisans had to be left behind for lack of weapons. ("If only we had had twenty more hand grenades . . .!")

At last, on July 26th of 1953, at the closing of Santiago's yearly carnival, 150 rebels with two girls for nurses and a physician, disguised themselves in army uniforms and stormed the island's second largest military encampment, the Moncada fort, headquarters of the 1,000 troops of the Maceo regiment. The plan was to infiltrate the installation, hold the soldiers at bay and seal the arsenal to prevent its being used against the people, while another contingent would take over the post's radio station and broadcast an appeal to the citizenry urging them to join the insurrection.

But for a couple of mishaps they might have succeeded. For one, the car transporting their heavy weapons got lost in the departing throngs of carnival and failed to arrive in time. As it turned out, the attack on Fort Moncada was the Revolution's first major setback and perhaps its finest hour. The magnitude of the enterprise and the courage and ideals which had inspired it shook the lethargic people out of their apathy and vulcanized them into protest, underground resistance, and eventually into overt action.

As in every revolution, the price was high. Half of the rebels died, not in combat, but under torture. Their captors were eager to pin the blame for the aborted insurrection on some high official or foreign instigator. The irate tyranny could not conceive that the near-defeat it suffered had been inflicted by a group of ill-equipped youthful civilians with no ties whatsoever to disgruntled politicians, army chiefs, or an exotic ideology. There simply was nothing to confess to, and the truth was too compromising for the government, too indicative of oppression and discontent to be admitted.

The revenge of the armed forces and the embarrassed dictator was to surpass the savagery of the Machado dictatorship of the twenties. One of the voices who speak to us in this book is that of a living martyr of the Moncada atrocities. From an adjoining cell she was forced to hear the agony of her brother and her fiancé as they died under questioning. At the end, in an effort to extract from her the information the victims had not revealed, she was shown the eyeball of one and the testicles of the other. Wanton murder of even innocent civilians became rampant in Cuba's eastern provinces.

Eventually, the fleeing hunted rebels and their leaders were caught and brought to trial. They received sentences ranging from five to fifteen years. But, from that defeat, the Revolution gained its Bill of Rights in the form of one of the most extraordinary documents of our time: Fidel Castro's own defense. After being held incommunicado for 76 days, denied the use of books and legal papers and counsel, aided only by a privileged memory, he gave a devastating dissertation in which he reviewed the human and legal rights of men to rebel against tyrannical lords, from the struggles of Oliver Cromwell against Charles I, to the American and the French Revolutions. He quoted from the Rights of Man and the American Declaration of Independence, from the writings of Rousseau, Milton, Balzac, Locke, Saint Thomas Aquinas, José Martí . . . Turning against his captors he indicted them for abetting the inhumanity and corruption of the dictatorship. He reviewed Cuba's chronic social injustices and economic ills; 33% illiteracy, 30% unemployment, the majority of the people living in hovels, sustaining themselves on a diet of roots and rice, unable to give their children shoes, medical care, a hope, a skill, a future. This in the middle of one of Latin America's most prosperous 'democracies,' where customarily government officials took office as paupers and finished their term as millionaires.

In the presence of the 100 soldiers guarding him in that courtroom, Fidel Castro accused Batista of a reign of terror and illegality which left the people no other course to liberation than a civilian uprising. And instead of asking for an acquittal, he closed his defense by demanding to be sent to join his brother-rebels already serving jail terms in the Isle of Pines prison, ending with these prophetic words: "Sentence me, it does not matter. History will absolve me."

With the text of the speech circulating in Cuba and even abroad, with the Moncada atrocities coming to light day by day, public sentiment rose to a point that Batista was forced to yield to the cries demanding amnesty for the young prisoners or risk further unrest, the last thing he wanted his American sponsors to know. Before setting them free, every attempt was made by the regime to corrupt the rebels with offers of government jobs and private enterprises. Not one of them accepted. Instead they drafted and signed a joint statement asserting their position. ("It seems that there will be an amnesty for us if we make a tacit agreement to respect the illegal regime in power by force in the Republic. The cynics who suggest such things believe that after twenty months in prison we have lost our integrity under the hardships that have been imposed upon . . . We can be deprived of our rights by force, but nobody will succeed in persuading us to return to freedom by offering us an unworthy accord, gifts, or jobs . . . We will not yield one atom of our honor in exchange for freedom . . . We hereby refuse to accept an amnesty at the price of dishonor. Our spirit is undaunted. We will bear our fate with courage and remain as a living indictment of the tyranny.") They won, on their terms. Shortly after the amnesty they went into self-imposed exile in Mexico, there to reorganize and begin training for another try.

By the winter of 1956 the rebels felt ready for "an invasion." The quotes are meant to be ironic. How can one seriously call the arrival of a rickety old yacht with 82 ill-equipped civilians *an invasion*? The odyssey of that landing and the rebel's ascent to the Sierra Maestra are superbly told by journalist Robert Taber in his book *M-26*, the best history of the Cuban insurrection in English, French or Spanish. The historic pilgrimage was as tragic as the attack on Fort Moncada. Only 12 men made it to the summit of the Sierra, the rest got shot or captured by the army and the air force. But the outcome was a miracle. With those twelve hunted, lost, dogtired men Fidel began his actual war against Batista. Nearly a month after the landing, sustaining themselves on raw turtles and land-crabs, extracting dew from leaves for moisture, they reached the highest point in the island, the Turquino peak, on the eve of December 25th. ("It's Christmas, Fidel. Do you know that?" "I do. The days of the tyranny are numbered.")

Entrenched in the jungles, hills and maniguas of the Sierra they gathered peasants to their cause and made contact with their awaiting partisans in the cities. The urban resistance was being led by 24 year old Frank País, until he was shot dead b ythe police in one of Santiago's colonial streets. His name and exploits are mentioned with love and reverence in this book. We also hear some of the voices recall the adventures of many girls of Santiago who served as couriers and suppliers to the rebels, remaining with them between trips to man rifle and submachine gun in combat and guard duty. One of them, Vilma Espín, a young architect, even had a prize of several thousand dollars offered by Batista for her head, escandalizing Santiago's society of which her family were prominent members. She was hidden by friends and relatives, and today, as Mrs. Raúl Castro, she is the mother of four as well as one of the top officials of the Revolutionary government.

Another girl who made history with her courage and dedication is Celía Sánchez, daughter of a well-known physician of Oriente province. As Fidel's inseparable companion and confidant, she is one of the most important figures of the Revolution which she serves as Secretary of the Council of Ministers.

One wonders how this slender, elegant young woman could be the alert, boots-and-fatigue clad sniper one sees in the photos taken of the rebels during the hard days in the Sierra.

For two years the rebels fought Batista's armed forces in the mountains. They also had time to set up a mobile hospital where many peasants received medical aid and even surgical attention for the first time. They established their own broadcasting station, *Radio Rebelde,* which kept the island informed of war developments and watever was safe to tell about guerrilla life. ("Mama, this is Pepito. Don't worry, I'm fine," one was likely to hear between news, Martí poems, and Guantanameras.) They printed their own letterpress newspaper, *Sierra Maestra,* copies of which have become collectors' items. They even had their own chaplain, officiating on a portable altar on 'quiet' days. "We married countless peasants and baptized their children, often at the same ceremony," he told me when we met in 1964. His name was Father Guillermo Sardiñas—Major Sardiñas when he would don boots and uniform—a scholarly priest who had joined the Underground in 1953 when he was chaplain of the Isle of Pines prison where the rebels served twenty months of their incomplete sentences. He never left them since. Until his fatal heart attack two years ago, Father Sardiñas was Chaplain General of the Cuban Rebel Army and probably the first priest in the world to wear an olive-green cassock with the insignias of a major pinned to it next to the cross and the Sacred Heart. The friendship he dispensed me during the four weeks I last spent in Cuba was one of the memorable encounters I've had with the paradoxical and often misunderstood Cuban Revolution.

Not all the spisodes recalled in this book take place in the Sierra Maestra. One of the most moving chapters refers to the attack on Havana's presidencial palace on March 13th, 1957, when a group of university students attempted to shorten the war and stop bloodshed by abducting Batista and forcing his resignation. As told here by one of the survivors, it reads like a British spy-thriller but for the sublimity of the purpose and the pathetic outcome.

Another chapter evokes Camilo Cienfuegos' campaign in the province of Las Villas, with the accent of a tropical Good Private Schweik that is a joy to read. For some inexplicable reason—least of all for space considerations in this far from lengthy book—the translator has omitted some important portions of the original, and Camilo's chapter is one of the most affected by this arbitrary editing.

But . . . good enough. As the accents, the humor, the pathos and sublimity of these conversations delight or move or infuriate us, history unfolds before us in this book; undistorted by subsequent political expediencies, unshadowed by the more imponderable events that were to come. This is how the Cuban Revolution started, bizarre, paradoxical or quixotic as it may seem, misunderstood and advisedly ill-interpreted as it often has been by a large sector of the American press even before U.S. antagonism, attacks and eventual blockade led Cuba to seek alliances of defense and supply with the Soviet Union.

The origin was as simple and homegrown as you will read it in Carlos Franqui's THE TWELVE: the disenfranchised youth of a nation rising against cyclopean odds to rescue their people from hunger and oppression, and doing it in the only way known to them, in the tradition of the great liberators of their continent; Washington, Bolívar, Sncre, Morelos, San Martín, Miranda, José Martí . . .

In these cynical times that style may seem archaic, romantic, too idealistic. Yet, it continues to be a singularly positive one in underdeveloped Latin America, for it rests precisely on the thorough identification of the leader with the needs and aspirations and the grassroots idiom of the masses he will lead in that particular area, a leader who pronounces the cry for liberty and plunges physically into battle at the head of his troops, the first to fight, often the first to die as in the case of Martí and Guevara.

The image of the inspired and usually scholarly liberator—poet, farmer, doctor, lawyer, priest or soldier—marching at the head of his rebels to fight a tyranny which surpasses them in all but in purity of ideals and human needs, continues to have a magical appeal for the impassioned youth and destitute peasantry of Latin America. How can a cold scientific plan devised in some remote land compete with that historical and practical reality? Be it the United States, Russia or China that does the devising. All three are equally foreign and unidentified with the Latin American masses and their homegrown leaders. Whether benevolent or sinister, such plans simply do not work in Iberian Indo-America as they may with more docile, less culturally defined Eastern European and Asiatic masses.

The Cuban Revolution was and remains eminently Cuban, despite the necessary political alliances of the present. One century of American economic domination and cultural penetration meant nothing in Cuba when time came for liberation, and there is reason to believe that the Russians are not having more of an impact. With pertinent regional adaptations, whether to the Andes or the Caribbean, such an indigenous Latin American movement cannot help fire and inspire the Latin American masses a lot more than the distant blueprints and computations of Washington or Moscow. Thus the Alliance for Progress is destined to remain suspect in Latin America, a foreign plot to be taken advantage of but never to inspire one ounce of idealism even in those few of the masses who benefit by it. In that respect, we are not even fooling some of the people most of the time.

To ignore that practical and historical reality is what leads a pragmatic, guilt-ridden United States—where by now 'freedom' is only a slogan to mask the legendary American quest for expansionism—to label every tremor of national liberation in underdeveloped countries with the convenient epithet of communist, or communist-inspired. In doing so we only pay communism an undue compliment, as if Man's need for bread, land, jobs, health education and dignity were the exclusive discovery of communism. The hungry and destitute peoples of the world hardly need Marxist scholars to point the way towards justice and human fulfillment, whether in Batista's Cuba, in today's Vietnams, Bolivias, Harlems or Angolas. And that way, as consistently shown even in modern history, is not the 'gradual' parliamentary or electoral process so cherished by those least disposed to accept a sharing of material blessings, by whatever means. The way, in our times from June 17, 1775 in Bunker Hill to July 26, 1953 in Santiago, is armed revolt.

This is how Cuba did it, here in the voices of Carlos Franqui's book, THE TWELVE.

New York, December 1967   Tana de Gámez

PREFACE

This is history as recounted by the participants themselves with the aid of a microphone and of a questioning reporter who was reasonably well-informed of the situations described.

The accounts were recorded at war's end, before repetition had turned them stale, recorded so that history might emerge from the dialogue fresh, alive and spontaneous. There is not a word here which was not first spoken aloud. We had the participants speak as if they were engaged in direct conversation with you in your own living room.

As a camera films all before it, so our recording equipment registered everything without time considerations. The transcription has not been rewritten and it should be read always keeping in mind how time unrolls in real conversations.

Each speaker describes what struck him most in his own experience, which is to say, each in the story speaks for himself. Thus are these days reconstructed.

Almost all the stories center on events at the beginning of the war. Without our having sought such an emphasis, the speakers tell principally of happenings between December 2, 1956—when the yacht *Granma* landed with eighty-two men on the south coast of Oriente Province—and the battle at El Uvero, May 28, 1957.

This book is called *The Twelve* because after the initial disaster there were twelve men left who, beaten and cornered by thousands of Batista troops, persisted in continuing the fight which brought victory two years later.

The story of the Twelve has now become legend. They speak here through five of them who recount their experiences.

You will also find in the book other personal stories told by the first two peasants to join with the Twelve, by three women who took part in the struggle, and by two city men who participated in the attack on the presidential palace at Havana on March 13, 1957. There is an account of events toward the end of the war showing how a column of eighty-two men, directed by one of the Twelve, crossed over six hundred miles of enemy-held territory, and there is the story of Frank País' death at Santiago de Cuba. Finally, in the women's accounts appears the master thread, going all the way from July 26, 1953 to January 1, 1959, that is, from the beginning to the end of the war.

All the accounts focus on military action, but there are moments in which the familiar mixes with the heroic. Intimate details, bits of daily life, humor, jumping around—that's the Cuban way of telling a story.

Characters of the book in order of appearance, of whom the first four were Rebel Comandantes, a rank approximating that of major in most armies:

EFIGENIO AMEJEIRAS: One of the Twelve. Second in command to Raul Castro in the advance of the Second Front begun March 10, 1958. Lost three brothers in war: Juan Manuel, in attack on Moncada Barracks, July 26, 1953; Gustavo, murdered in a Batista prison; and Machaco, killed in Havana in a building while battling the police. First Chief of Revolutionary Police. Born in Havana. Formerly a chauffeur.

JUAN ALMEIDA: Veteran of the Moncada attack, made prisoner with Fidel Castro, jailed on the Isle of Pines, exiled in Mexico after the amnesty, member of the *Granma's* expeditionary force, one of the Twelve, first lieutenant to Fidel in Sierra Maestra, Cuban hero, wounded several times. After war be-

came and remains Chief of Rebel Army. Negro, born
in Havana, was a bricklayer.

JOSE PONCE: Veteran of Moncada and *Granma.*
Burned by napalm. First imprisoned at Moncada, then
sent to the Isle of Pines for two years. A designer,
born at Artemisa in Pinar del Río Province.

UNIVERSO SANCHEZ: Member of *Granma* expedition. One of two men with Fidel Castro after raid
at Alegría del Pío on December 4, 1956, when Fidel
was encircled and hunted by Batista troops. Veteran
of Sierra campaign and leader of a Rebel column.
Peasant, born in Matanzas Province.

CELIA SANCHEZ: Organizer, along with Frank
País, of the 26th of July Movement in cities, and of
group awaiting Fidel at time of landing. Veteran of
Sierra Maestra, Fidel's principal aide in war and peace.
Born at Manzanillo (Oriente Province) of a well-to-do
family.

HAYDEE SANTAMARIA (often called Yeyé): One
of the two women (the other was Melba Hernández)
who took part in the attack on Moncada Barracks.
While she was prisoner, Batista's torturers showed
her the eyes of her brother Abel—second in command
of assault groups—and the testicles of her fiancé,
Boris Santa Coloma. Veteran of Sierra and city warfare. Married to Armando Hart, a battle comrade now
a government official. Born to a middle-class family
at Las Villas.

GUILLERMO GARCIA and MANUEL FAJARDO:
The first two peasants to join up with Fidel, active
participants in the war; Guillermo as Chief of the

Army of Occidente; Manuel in charge of cattle-raising on Turiguano Island (Camagüey Province). Both formerly small farmers of Sierra Maestra.

FAURE CHOMON: Founder, with Jose Echevarría, of Revolutionary Directorate. A leader of the attack on the presidential palace, veteran of Escambray. Formerly a student. Born in Camagüey.

LUIS GOICOCHEA: Sole survivor of the group which infiltrated Batista's office during the attack on the palace. Escambray veteran. Born in Havana, was a worker before the war.

CAMILO CIENFUEGOS: Underground militant, wounded in student demonstration, *Granma* veteran. One of the Twelve. Leader of the column that marched across the island of Cuba. Wounded in combat, hero of the Revolution. Disappeared at sea aboard a Crespa plane during a stormy night, October 28, 1959. Had been a clerk, was born at Havana.

VILMA ESPIN: Director, with Frank País, of the attack on Santiago, November 30, 1956. Combatant on the Second Front, aide to Raul Castro, whom she married at war's end. Currently president of the Federation of Cuban Women. Architect from a wealthy Santiago family.

Carlos Franqui

Chapter One

FOUR COMANDANTES TALK IT OVER

ALMEIDA: I met Efigenio in Mexico. He had just come from San José, Costa Rica. It must have been six in the afternoon and Efigenio was neat as a pin, wearing a blue suit, a white shirt and black shoes. He was waiting for me near a *tacos* seller's stand. A *taco* over there, that's a kind of pancake of rolled corn flour with fried pork inside it.

Ponce I knew about the time of Moncada. He'd already recovered from a bullet wound in the lungs received in that attack. Now he was much better. He was a little tricky, got a kick out of keeping secrets

21

from comrades. And me, I used to be a regular comedian. That's why we got along so well: you know, between artists. . . .

PONCE: During the attack on Moncada, we were in different spots. I was in one of the first cars. Others were assigned to take over the nearby hospital. Moncada brought people together from many places. Afterwards, too—in prison.

In the house at the suburb of Siboney, before the attack, there was a mess of unknown faces. In fact, nobody knew anybody else.

Here's how I joined the ranks of the Revolution. Or, rather, the insurrection, because back then I didn't know the meaning of revolution.

ALMEIDA: Let's begin at the beginning. I was a mason's helper. We had a workyard at Ayesterán. The boss was a good guy. Up to a point, anyway. Deep down he was decent but not about the job because, actually, he gave us starvation wages.

One day I got to know Comrade Armando Mestre, a high school student in Havana. A real sport. He lived near me and we got along well. We'd go out together and talk things over. He asked me if I was studying; I told him no, I'd quit school in the third grade and I didn't have a chance to keep up my studies. Then he said he'd try and help me so I could get back to school, because that would open up lots of things for me. I told him, sure, school would give me a lot but I had to make a living first, since I came from a big family and had to help my parents.

Our friendship had already lasted a few years when

Batista's coup came on March 10, 1952. Armando came to tell me, "Let's go to the University. They're mobilizing the people against this military coup and they are trying to save the country."

We went there. People were looking for weapons. There weren't any—weapons were coming, weapons weren't coming. . . . Finally, the first weapons I'd ever seen were the ones Fidel gave us in the Hall of Martyrs on University Hill, so that we could get the hang of the M-1. Springfields, too, but the M-1 without a stock or, I should say, with a removable stock, that was something everybody got to handle. Those were the rudimentary weapons with which we made our first steps, our first contact with firearms. Now, of course, everybody can use a gun.

Pedrito Miret was responsible for the meeting place. That padded jacket with an H sewed on it, do you remember it? And that gesture he had, snapping open his fist like that? And how he used to stamp his foot?

That's where I met Fidel. He began talking about the Revolution and explained the process of evolution and how the *coup d'etat* was a step backwards. He said that youth had to unite, that it was a vital force, that he was counting on elements which hadn't made any compromise with the past.

That was my first contact with Fidel. It wasn't long after March 10. He was always carrying a volume of Lenin under his arm. A blue book with a picture of Lenin in relief on the cover. He wore a grey suit, a well-used shirt with a worn collar. He always had that same energetic way about him.

PONCE: Fidel? The first time I came in contact with him I already knew Pepe Suárez, who organized the 26th of July Movement at Artemisa. I had a small printshop in Artemisa which was called *Hermanos Ponce*. A little place with a number 4 machine.

Well, there was Batista's coup and March 11, in the morning, some students came to get a manifesto printed by us. I did print it, and put at the bottom the *Hermanos Ponce* label. They paid me and I went back to my work.

At lunchtime I always went for my coffee to a café called the *Aurora*. And that's where I bumped into the corporal. You see, I am going to get my coffee and, when I pass by the bank, about forty yards from the café, I see something peculiar: the famous Corporal Frometa planted there, looking about, with some character who was pointing directly at me. I say to myself, "You're not running away. You're going to drink your coffee as if nothing's going on."

But when I pass him, he grabs me by the neck like that and gives me a blow in the back, then puts me in a car and we're on the way to the barracks. I remember Lieutenant Ruiz being there. I was thrown in a dungeon and got beaten up. The next day they let me out. From then on I spoke foul of Batista wherever I went.

One evening, after I was acquitted, I met Pepe Suárez in the park and he told me what was going on. He told me about Fidel, that he was young and had new ideas, and how the Movement had nothing to do with the past or with political hacks. So I said,

"Fine, keep me informed." One Saturday morning he came and said, "Tomorrow wait for me. We're going to Havana." That's all he told me.

We went to Havana, to the offices of the Orthodox Party, and that was my first contact with the comrades. I got to know Andres Luján and some of the others, too. That was the place where we received instructions from the University of Havana. Yes, Pedrito had a special habit. Always did this—a tight fist and then pop! he would open his hand. Every time he was going to laugh or exclaim something, he did it. We'd point it out and he'd turn red, annoyed.

All they had at the house on Prado Boulevard was a submachine gun and an M-1. At Artemisa some of us used to get together regularly also, but we never greeted each other in the streets. Our meetings took place at the Masonic lodge.

This was about the time I first saw Fidel. On the Central Highway, as I recall. Pepe Suárez said to me, "Stay in the car." An old jalopy. I found a book on the seat. It was by Martí.[1] It had a red cover and many of Martí's statements were underlined. Just then, Fidel, who had been in a house across the way, came over. That was in 1952.

In our group there were Ciro Redondo, Julio Díaz, Ricondo, Flores, and Labrador, a comrade who lost an eye in the attack on the Moncada Barracks.

And there were some comrades who later fell at

---

[1] José Martí (1853-1895), Cuban writer, revolutionary, champion of the struggle for liberty in all Latin America.

Moncada, like those peasants from Pijiriga. I don't remember their names any more because we didn't have much contact with them. Well, that's how it goes. . . .

Almeida I met at Boniato. In the prison at Boniato.

ALMEIDA: Yes. It was hard, those early days. But everybody understood what was going on: not one prisoner complained. The comrades helped each other and that was clear for all to see later in the courtroom. We were sentenced, some to ten years, others to three, in the penitentiary on the Isle of Pines. . . . And I remember that book of Lenin. It was the one they seized afterwards at Moncada.

In those days I was always smiling, always gay. I had a, well, let's say an easier outlook on life. I remember when I went for shooting practice at Los Palos. An instructor there was teaching us how to shoot with .22 rifles. They put up an empty milk can and each of us had to fire at it. Six shots. I took my rifle without ever having fired before and bang! the first shot hit the can! The second shot in the can, bang! the third in the can, bang! . . . I began to jump around like a goat, yelling, "I'm terrific, just terrific!" Then the instructor said, "Now, now, comrade, it's crazy to be excited like that!" And I answered him right back, "Nope, I'm happy inside, I can't hold it back." He said to me, "I don't think you're going to be much of a revolutionary." And me: "Listen to me—if I had been born in '95 I would have been a veteran of the War of Independence. Okay, in today's war I can only be a good revolutionary."

When we left for the attack on Moncada, a special recommendation was made about me. My dossier must have said I was a bit wacky, because Fidel said to Comrade Alcalde, who was driving the car to which I was assigned: "Keep on eye on Almeida, he's some kind of a joker."

They took me to Santiago on the Central Highway practically like they would a prisoner. Comrade Alcalde must have thought I was going to take off. The last thing in the world I'd want to do, since I thought we were driving to the carnival at Santiago as a reward for my doing so well in our training exercises.

We arrived in Santiago about four-thirty, the afternoon of the 25th. We went into a house at Celda Street, then left for another address where Comrade Guitart came about midnight to lead us away. He took us to Siboney, and there they started passing out uniforms. Uniforms of Batista's army.

"Great," I thought. "They're going to give me a rifle, aren't they?" I waited for my rifle like the Messiah. When I saw that the one they gave me was a .22-caliber I froze up. . . .

From the moment I arrived at Celda Street I knew it wasn't a training exercise this time, but a real revolutionary mission. But honestly, I have to tell you that when I saw that rifle my heart sank. It just about stopped. Imagine—a .22! They passed out the bullets and I took my four boxes. And I waited. Before leaving, Fidel spoke to the comrades about the historic event we were about to live through.

I don't remember his exact words very well. But I

do recall his saying that we would be remembered and even earn a well-deserved place in history books.

There were some comrades who had become frightened. Fidel gave them encouragement. For my part, I'd have shot them, because on account of them there was some confusion later on.

For the rest, all Cubans know what happened. The shooting, comrades killed, those who could manage it getting away, our stay in the mountains until August 1. . . .

Fidel, Alcalde and Pepe were captured in a hut. I was taken along with Mestre, Mario Chanes, Francisco González and Montané. Sarría's men made the captures.

Comrade Mestre, who has died since, got the worst manhandling. They kept telling him, "Come over here. *You* a revolutionary? Don't you know Negroes can't be revolutionaries? Negroes are either thieves or Batista's supporters, but never revolutionaries!" As for me, they threw me down on the ground. When I got up they fired over my head. I had to get back down and then they told me to get up—I didn't know what to do. Then Sarría came in and told me to stay on my feet.

AMEJEIRAS: You weren't afraid?

ALMEIDA: No, we weren't afraid. To tell the truth, numbness overtakes you in those cases, so you don't react to the danger. They loaded us on a truck, tied our hands, and took us to the bivouac area. There we met other men: Raul Castro, Ramiro Valdés and some whose names I've forgotten. Then there was the trial.

From the Boniato prison we were sent by plane to the Isle of Pines for twenty-two months. And that's where we were stuck, so I began trying to figure things out.

I found out I was an artist, a comedian! I'd wrap a scarf around my head, dress up like a woman, and put on a show. We often put together evening programs. One comrade would sing, there was a duet called "Chord and Butt," with Andrés García and Pedrito Miret.

AMEJEIRAS: What happened with Fidel one day when he was playing volley ball against Cartaya?

ALMEIDA: We had been beating them. He threw the ball so hard the umpire had to step in.

Ponce was kind. He was our letter writer. He used to tell us how to write love letters. Guys would consult him: "Tell me, Ponce, what should I write?" He was the prison scholar.

PONCE: No, that was Andrés.

ALMEIDA: Andrés and you. And you also sang.

PONCE: I sang only when they brought us some tobacco.

ALMEIDA: The *26th of July* anthem was composed at Boniato. By Comrade Cartaya.

Yes, we did have some funny volley ball games. Once I cut my hand playing. We really went at it! Sparta against Sparta!

Eventually they had an amnesty and released us. After that came new fear, misery and crises and uncertainties. Fidel was already gone. He had given the comrades orders to rejoin him one by one.

Then, thanks to Yeyé, who worked in José Manuel Gutiérrez' law office, and to Melba, I got a passport. The 17th of June I sailed on the *Andrea*. I arrived in Vera Cruz and took the train for Mexico City. There I had the joy of finding my battle comrades. Do you know what it's like, meeting fellow countrymen in a foreign country? We began shooting practice, telling ourselves each cartridge was paid for with the sweat and blood of comrades still in Cuba, Cubans who were sacrificing themselves to supply us with money. We knew we had to become crack shots, to be tops in our training exercises, so we could do what Fidel had promised the people when he said we would either be martyrs or heroes very soon.

We haven't talked about Amejeiras' story, his "Mau-Maus." That "Mau-Mau" story goes back to before the resistance in the Sierra Maestra.

AMEJEIRAS: Right. That was when you were on the Isle of Pines. The Mau-Maus was the little group fighting against Omar Borges, Max Lesnik and the leaders of the Orthodox Party's Youth Movement, because they were not supporting Fidel. They went so far as to denounce us in their newspaper. Talk about dirty tricks! They said we were rowdy elements, completely dedicated to insurrection and against peaceful solutions through elections. They said all that, right out in the open! It was signed by young leaders of the Orthodox Communist Party.

I knew about Fidel for a long time, like many other people, because he had distinguished himself so much as a student leader; and he had spoken on the radio against the crimes of the Prío government, which preceded Batista. But I was *personally* acquainted with him from the time I told you about, when Juan Manuel introduced him to me.

The second time I saw him was two or three days before the attack on the Moncada Barracks. I was coming back from work; I was chauffeur to the manager of a company that built radio batteries. I saw Fidel go in the house where my brother lived, he spoke to him, then left. It was a Sunday afternoon. You never saw Fidel for long—Sunday was as good a work day for him as any other.

Then we didn't see each other again until after the attack, when everybody had been arrested. . . .

We organized an action cell. From Prado Street we kept the flame of rebellion alive while you were in prison. We began throwing bombs, brought action into the streets, and joined in all the student demonstrations. Then you came out of prison. And Fidel decided to leave for Mexico because they were preparing an attack on him. They even had—I remember how people were saying—they even had a car already riddled with bullets so they could claim he had fired at the police and that is why they had to kill him.

Fidel had his own plans: he was leaving for Mexico. We had our instructions from the Movement leadership to continue the struggle in Havana. My brothers (Machaco, Salvador, Gustavo) and me. Gustavo was in charge of distributing propaganda in the provinces, while Machaco, Salvador and myself worked in Havana. But you never know what fate has in store for you. One day we had to get some weapons. It so happened that four comrades had taken refuge in the Haitian embassy. They were accused of plotting an assassination attempt on Batista, an attempt which failed, I think, because of Prío's getting cold feet and because of other troubles. Everything had been ready, but they hesitated, lost time, and the plot was discovered. Then a revolutionary comrade told me, "Listen, Efigenio, tonight we're going to the Haitian embassy. Nobody's on watch. We find the ambassador and tell him we're revolutionaries and that all he has to do is give us the four revolvers and four grenades our comrades had on them. That will give us weapons."

We agreed to do it, but when we arrived at the embassy two armed policemen came out of the garden, shouting, "Halt!" Well, we began explaining we were bus drivers and showed them our transit company cards. We had fake ones for our underground work. But the police didn't let us go, and one of them went to phone his station. A car came with a commander they called Chu-chu (Bang-bang) because he had been involved in all the shooting at the University. Even I recognized him from having seen him two or three times at demonstrations where he had been firing and doing worse things.

Well, he had arrived and the policemen told him, "Commander, we caught these two characters trying to find refuge in there!" He told them, "Get them in the car!" I knew what this could mean, especially to

me, the most compromised of the three, because someone in our group had given me away after our dynamite attacks. The police were looking for us, and also
Salas Cañizares' security men and the Department of
Special Revolutionary Investigations. That meant we
would be tortured to death at the precinct.

I pushed past a cop and slipped into the embassy.
The door happened to be open. The concierge, a Galician, told me, "You'll have to get out, you'll have to
get out!" I put my hand on my belt and snapped,
"Listen, Galician, I have just killed two or three men
in the street and I'll kill you instantly!" My Galician
got so frightened he ran and hid himself in the
kitchen. Of course, I wasn't armed at all. It was a
crazy bluff.

Then Comrades Israel Escalona, El Guajiro (you
knew him, "Crazy" Casanova), Julio César and Ernesto
Carbonell, they told me they didn't know where to
go, they were in trouble for being mixed up in the
Goicuría matter and had to get into the embassy building. So we decided to keep the guards pleasantly occupied; some girls from the University came over and
began chatting with the guards while our pals slipped
over the wall in back of the embassy. About ten of
them.

A few days later I was on my way to Costa Rica,
because we were refused visas for Haiti. As soon as I
got to San José, I made the acquaintance of Comrade
Ponce, who was keeping himself busy there, along
with another comrade, Gustavo Arcos.

It wasn't a very good situation. No, we really didn't

have many *colones*. The *colón*, that's Costarican money.

Well, Comrade Ponce noticed that they didn't have sandals with wooden soles in San José, didn't use them for slippers or anything. He said to me, "I think we could open a little sandal factory here." Maybe he had a good idea, if business went well we'd make the money to reach Mexico. So we got our workshop going: a file, some wood and an old tire. We cut up the tire and attached strips of it to wood pieces. The shop was called *José Ponce and Company*.

After we produced the first two dozen pairs we talked things over. The manufacturing had gone well; we worked in the courtyard of our boarding house where nobody could see us. But Ponce didn't want to go out and sell the sandals because he had a girl friend and he didn't like the idea of her seeing him peddling. I didn't want anybody to see me any more than he did. As for Gustavo, he wouldn't even hear of his doing it. Finally, though, each of us had to go out in turn with the two dozen pairs. We went around San José but sold only one dozen. So we started to leave them at boarding houses, saying, "Try them and we'll come back later." When we left for Cuba another Cuban, Manolito Carbonell's father, took over the factory, but he didn't give us anything for it.

ALMEIDA: The factory! You mean the woodpile.

AMEJEIRAS: No, the file—the factory was the file and the tire.

Well, Comrade Ponce had solved his passport problem—they'd given him a visa. I went to the Mexican embassy but they refused me mine. Two or three days later I went back and offered some money to an official. You know, there's always someone on the take end. I offered him twenty-five dollars and he said, "Good, come back tomorrow for your visa." I told myself it was in the bag.

And I told Gustavo, "I'm going to solve my problem by greasing the palm of an official at the Mexican embassy. When I give him twenty-five dollars, he gets me the visa."

Gustavo was indignant. "That's a shame! First they refuse you the visa and now they'll give it to you for a bribe!" He wanted to expose the crook—Gustavo's like that, all integrity.

"Wait a minute," I told him, "you'll wreck everything! Leave that Mexican official alone, otherwise I won't be able to leave."

The next day I went to the embassy. I don't know what happened, but now the character refused me the visa. Nothing doing. Why? A mystery. I think some informers denounced us. They had already told the police we were training on Sundays with Garands and M-3 rifles, under a Costarican lieutenant. They had even told where. But we were warned, and the Sunday when the police counted on catching us, we didn't show up.

So there was no way to leave any more. I saw myself forced to settle in San José. Then I had an idea that was at least halfway good. I asked Gustavo, who's now ambassador to Belgium, for some money, then went downtown. There I sat on a bench and waited. When I saw a shoeshine boy who was thin, like me, I called him over to shine my shoes. Then I asked him if he wanted to make some easy money.

"Doing what? Is it dangerous?" he asked.

"There's no danger."

"Good. What do I have to do? And how much will I make?"

"You'll make fifty dollars."

"*Fifty* dollars?" You can imagine—down there a dollar was worth twelve *colones* or so. "What do I have to do?"

"Just the following—get all the papers necessary to get a passport; when you have your passport, along with a visa, you'll bring them to me, I'll give you the money and leave for Mexico. When I arrive I'll send you fifty dollars more." Of course, I had no intention of doing that but I wanted to keep him hungry so after he got paid, he wouldn't go and denounce me.

All right. We got the papers together. That took us three days. Then we went to the embassy. But, because this guy had a record from when he was a kid, I think, and the cops used to keep an eye on him, they got suspicious. And also, they had seen him talking to me. I waited for him in front of the embassy. When he came out I asked, "Well?" Looking satisfied, he gave me the passport. I leafed through it and saw the visa for Mexico was there. At that moment, wham! four inspectors fell on us and took us into custody.

At the police station, you know what it's like. Caught with somebody else's passport. They asked if

I was planning to leave the country with it. Of course, at first I denied that. Then I decided to tell the truth. The lieutenant who was questioning me asked if I belonged to the Prío group. I told him I didn't. I was with the 26th of July Movement, directed by Fidel Castro.

Well, this fellow thought for a while, then he said, "Let's face it. You are declaring you're not with Prío's men. And yet you were going to take part in an assassination attempt against the ambassador of the Batista government in San José!"

I told him there was some mistake. True, there had been a little disturbance the day the ambassador presented his credentials, because we had gathered in the street outside the government building for a peaceful protest, carrying some signs. The minister of Foreign Relations, Valverde, who came out looking like a janitor, had rolled up his sleeves and given Manolito Carbonell's father a slap. I slapped him back, not knowing who he was. Then a bunch of policemen fell on us. That was the extent of the disturbance from which I had managed to get away. I'd been hiding in the boarding house, and the next morning they seized me with the passport.

I figured I was sunk. I kept telling myself, "Between the trouble with the Minister and my fake passport—!" I stayed in prison all morning without eating a thing, I was so upset. Toward noon the lieutenant came to my cell. His name was Vargas. A lieutenant or captain, can't remember any more. A short fellow, friendly. He said to me, "Look, kid, tell me the truth. What did you want to do with the passport?"

"Okay, I'll tell you," I said. "It's to go to Mexico. They refuse to give me a visa, which by the way is completely illegal to refuse me. I am Cuban, in Fidel Castro's camp. Fidel is in Mexico and you know he has said publicly that he'll return to Cuba. When and how I can't tell you. Anyway, I don't know the details myself."

"Very good," he nodded. "Exactly what do you want?"

"To get to Mexico and rejoin Fidel. That's all. What will come after, the whole world will hear about it some day."

"I've read some articles by that lawyer," that's what he called Fidel, "in *Bohemia Magazine* and I sympathize with him. I think he's a clean-cut guy, young, decent and not tied up with the old-time politicians. I've seen plenty of those Prío characters around here; most of them are gangsters. I tell you in all sincerity—I can see the 26th of July people are morally superior: a handful of revolutionaries who have experienced pain and hunger here in San José. Well, what do you say if I let you go, just like that, and take you to the airport? You can get the first plane for Mexico. You have money for a ticket?"

I couldn't believe my ears. I wanted to throw my arms around him and kiss him. I replied, "I won't make you tell me twice. Let's go right away to the ticket office!"

"Let's get going." At the ticket office he told me,

"Fine. Tomorrow morning, wait for me at the airport."

The next day I was there. I presented my passport with the photo of my shoeshine man and they didn't even look at it. "Comrade" Vargas must have spread the word!

So we left San José for Mexico City. En route, Gustavo said, "Your troubles begin when we get to Mexico City because, no matter how thin you are, that guy on your passport doesn't look like you at all. If they start making a fuss over it, you have only one course open to you, make a really big uproar over it, say you're a political exile coming from San José where they wouldn't let you leave. In short, make a big noise to call public attention and see if somebody doesn't come forward to help."

I tried shrugging it off. "Actually there's nothing to worry about. Let's keep cool."

Then Gustavo had an idea. "Here's something— you have your vaccination certificate. Well, at Immigration that's the first thing they look at. Put your certificate on top so they don't have to open the passport to look for it."

When we got to Mexico City and our turn came, a lady dressed in white asked me for my certificate and an officer took my passport. He glanced down without opening it and passed it to the woman. She inspected the certificate, okayed it and that was that.

Gustavo was dragging his feet at the airport. I told him, "Gustavo, stop hanging around, let's hurry. I still can't believe we're in Mexico."

"Wait, I want to buy a magazine and a newspaper."

"Let's go! We'll end up getting arrested. A taxi and full speed ahead!" That's how we arrived at the house and that afternoon I met all those who were already there a long while.

The first day I went to see a bullfight. I believe it was a Sunday. The next day I went out to the ranch where we got our training.

People have never mentioned it but it is true: in Mexico Raul learned how to bullfight. He used to wave a jacket while someone pretended to be the bull. Maria-Antonia for example. At that time Universo was responsible for keeping watch at the ranch.

ALMEIDA: That's right. Then they sent him somewhere else with Bayo and I was put in charge of the 26th of July house. Universo wore a blue overcoat. He looked like a millionaire.

AMEJEIRAS: I believe I first got to know Universo the day I was with Fidel on that plantation in Cuba. On board the *Granma* I didn't recognize anybody. I was half-dead from seasickness.

PONCE: The first time I saw him, I didn't know it was Universo. That was in Mexico City by the Monument of the Revolution where there was a very pretty girl selling something. I said to myself, "That fellow has to be a Cuban."

UNIVERSO: The Movement had ordered me over to Cuba, then to come back. On the boat there were five comrades, among them Ciro Redondo. Raul was waiting for us at Veracruz. Five of us, but we only got to know each other on the dock when Raul called us together. But I already knew there had to be some compatriots aboard because everywhere I saw paper strips pasted up. The little flyers said things like, "We will be free or we will be martyrs." That was one of the big slogans at the time.

I began to prepare myself for sabotage and street fighting. I was to go back to Cuba with Nico López. I took a special one-month course to become a specialist in dynamite and all kinds of city-fighting. And then one day Fidel told me he had decided that I should stay longer in Mexico. The Movement complained, and Faustino too. As for me, I was not unhappy about staying. I did what I had to do and gladly.

Well, once we arrived in Veracruz we talked things over with Raul. Fidel was waiting for us at a trolley stop. I already knew him from Havana.

Back in the days when Almeida and the others were prisoners, after Moncada, I had begun organizing committees for the liberation of the political prisoners, in Matanzas Province. We waited for them when they were released but, naturally, I did not know them personally. I greeted them but they didn't have any idea who I was.

Eventually, I made contact with Fidel and paid him a visit. With Pedrito Miret we had the start of a movement aimed at wiping out Batista, some weapons and five radios. I'd also been in touch with someone who could help, an army sergeant, and I took Fidel to meet him. Yes, from the first moment I saw Fidel I knew he was solid like rock. "There's a completely reliable man," I told myself. "You have to be with him."

I began seeing Fidel every week. At his place I used to meet students. Already Fidel treated me like a friend and we used to talk hours at a time, even the whole night through. I remember one day when their electricity was cut off because they hadn't paid. I had some pesos and lent them the money.

It was at Numbers 25 and 12, facing the cemetery. Oh no, at 23 and 18. That was where Lydia Castro lived. The apartment faced the street. Fidel would be talking to students and young people. He was mobilizing them. I told myself, "He'll fight, this one will."

I had wanted to be in the Moncada attack. I kept up with things. The day they left, I was in the cafe Macanas. Mario Muñoz was supposed to come and get me. Muñoz was a good pal, kept me more or less up to date on what was doing. He sent people to look for me, but they didn't find me. It was a Friday.

He instructed a comrade, Gustavo Hernández, to tell me they were going off somewhere. I took it to mean Camagüey and also that we should seize the radio station. Five of us joined together, took some coffee and tobacco, and near the airport during the night we got hold of a car to go seize the radio station at Colón and stir up the area the day of the attack on Moncada. When morning came, there was no news of anything, so we left directly for Moncada itself. But the attack was already over, a flop. I was caught after almost getting there, arrested at Santiago.

Where I was held they killed plenty of the boys.

They'd say, "You there, come here!" Then they'd take them out and shoot them. There were prisoners covered with blood, leg wounds, all kinds of wounds. Nine of us had been spared. Me, the four in the car with me and four others—the only ones.

I'll tell you exactly what happened at La Plata[1]. When we decided to attack we picked up two peasant guides en route. They had some jars of honey. Fidel bought the honey and we shared it. As a bee keeper, I always said honey was very nourishing. Well, we got near the barracks area and I climbed up a tree. I spent the whole day perched there, watching soldiers with a telescope, and I kept telling Fidel what I saw.

ALMEIDA: We were the ones who spotted Frigate 106 through a telescope. You were with the scouting patrol.

UNIVERSO: Right—but I did spend that whole day up a tree, passing on information to Fidel, "They're doing such and such. . . . Now they're getting into firing position. Some are setting up empty cans. . . ." The cans went flying. Every time one of them fired a can fell. The men were shooting like the devil. They were in training.

Fidel decided to try some night ambushes in order to bring in people we could question. They sent me out with Crespo. We stopped a man with a boy. They told us that farther back Osorio was coming along, and that Osorio was a filthy rat, the worst of the bunch informing the army on the peasants.

[1] Battle of La Plata, January 17, 1957.

Then we waited for Osorio. He came on a mule. The peasant instantly pointed him out to us, "That's him!" We called out, "Halt there! Rural Guards!" He replied, "Mosquito!" That was the army password. I jumped him and grabbed his revolver, then we led him to Fidel. We were pretending to be Batista soldiers. Fidel pretended to be a colonel, or a major, a Batista officer sent there to conduct an investigation. Osorio began saying nasty things about soldiers who were really behaving well (there were some soldiers who didn't abuse people), and telling us good things about certain peasants and bad things about others. Whenever he spoke well about somebody we figured it had to be a dirty dog, and when he spoke badly about another man we knew he must be a good guy.

Afterwards, we tied him up and got closer to the military post. We came to a road. There was a thick fog. A corporal, Corporal Basol, passed by with some prisoners, peasants. He was saying, "Keep marching or I'll—" He went on threatening them. The peasants had been picked up because an uprising was feared.

PONCE: They were being taken to El Macho.

UNIVERSO: Later we learned that the soldiers killed them. Well, we decided against making a grab for the corporal. Too risky even for the poor peasants. He was on horseback and they were on foot, tied to the horse.

In the morning we set out again. Let's say the soldiers' barracks were here, then the marines' were there, and over here was a shed, very close, almost touching one of the barracks. And we were here, less than thirty yards away from that shack.

AMEJEIRAS: No, it wasn't like that!

UNIVERSO: It was, man. When I arrived—

ALMEIDA: I came through the main gate of the military post. I was the one there!

AMEJEIRAS: Universo, you weren't there, you couldn't remember that side. I was there with Almeida, Raul and his men. You others weren't there!

UNIVERSO: Let me explain to you. Look at the layouts: Fidel is here, right? Okay, I'm *there!* Let me speak!

AMEJEIRAS: I want you to say what's right, old pal.

UNIVERSO: I say things the way I remember them. Like you—right? Here there was a grove of carob-trees. Over here or there, not sure any more. The guard post was there, as the guide had told us. Fidel had let go a burst with his Thompson and wounded a guard. Then we all started firing at the buildings, shouting, "Surrender!" But nobody was surrendering. We lacked ammunition. Julio Díaz came running to me, saying, "Give me some bullets!" I gave him two of mine. I only had nine left. Then Fidel said, "Universo, the building must be set on fire!" He had already told me, "Throw your grenades!" I had one incendiary and two ordinary grenades plus two petards in my knapsack. When I'd thrown the incendiary, Fidel roared at me, "Throw it!" "I have thrown it!" "No, you haven't thrown it!"

Then I showed him the pin I'd pulled. Well, none of those grenades exploded because they had been buried too long in Santiago. So I lighted the fuse of each petard and threw them against the building. They didn't explode either—they, too, had been in damp ground.

He gave me a box of matches and I crawled forward to set the fire going that way. I wanted to start it in the thatch roof, *not* with a torch as some artist has drawn it in *Mella* magazine, but with a simple match. From a nearby building Sergeant Walter was shooting at me. I did my best to keep under cover because the place was full of soldiers firing away now. But I could not get the roof burning because the cover of palm thatch was too thick. Then Luís Crespo got there, dug into the thatch with a rifle butt and started a fire in the trough.

At that moment Che reached our side. A soldier came running out. Luís fired and the soldier fell. Che rushed toward him, grabbed his cartridges and turned him over on his back. The soldier cried out, "Don't kill me!" Che told him, "Stay still. The doctor will be here soon." Che took cover behind the guy and began shooting at the house.

Che once said that I went to set the house on fire and wasn't able to do it. And now *Mella* in its pages has picked up what Che said. But it isn't true. The truth is that between Crespo and myself we did get the place on fire.

Well, Fidel told me, "Run and tell the men to advance. If they don't advance now they'll have to retreat!" They did advance but I had to go tell them twice.

That was the attack on La Plata. We infiltrated the barracks and with Raul and another man forced the guards out, then we set it on fire. I say it because I know very well what I did and what Raul, who was commanding, did.

ALMEIDA: I seized three rifles, slung them on my back and ran back out!

UNIVERSO: I didn't say that I alone did everything.

ALMEIDA: There was Crescencio's son also.

AMEJEIRAS: It was Manuel Acuña who told them, "Surrender!" And a guard answered, "Nobody can surrender. Those who aren't dead are seriously wounded." That's what happened on the other side. We didn't see what Universo has been talking about because he was with Fidel and Che.

UNIVERSO: Che was not with me. He was with Calixto García. I was with Fidel and a comrade I've forgotten. I don't know if it was Fajardo or another guy.

AMEJEIRAS: Motova was with you. Do you remember? He captured a Thompson.

UNIVERSO: On my side we were three, that's all. Fidel had posted us, he in the middle, me here and the other guy there. I'm pretty certain it was Manuel Fajardo. That's the real story of the battle at La Plata.

AMEJEIRAS: There was the boy from Manzanillo killed by a mortar shell. He began tapping away at the shell and it went off, killing him.

UNIVERSO: Fidel has put it well, he said we should write history the way it is, no? Okay, there's your history, gentlemen.

AMEJEIRAS: The front of the barracks, the main entrance, it was Almeida who attacked it with a group. The two groups entered there. Almeida and Raul's.

ALMEIDA: There were two barracks and *two* attacking groups. Each had one barracks as its target. They attacked the palm-thatched one. We were busy with the more elaborately built structure, the one for the marines.

UNIVERSO: One of the barracks suffered more damage than the other. You, everybody had gone elsewhere. We riddled them with bullets.

AMEJEIRAS: Our barracks was solid wood and we were just a few yards away with our 30-06 guns. Figure it out for yourself: we were firing close to the ground. Those characters were wide open for us, literally they got torn to pieces.

In my group we had Raul Castro, who was in command, and Armando Rodríguez (he captured a Lewis gun), Ciro Redondo and myself.

UNIVERSO: There was also Julito Díaz, near the lemon grove.

AMEJEIRAS: Not Julito—Edward. I got a clear view of Almeida firing at the front of the barracks. He was shooting a submachine gun. And it was Manuel Acuña who stopped shooting to say, "Don't fire any more. They're screaming and moaning in there." He got near to the door and fired inside at one of the few men who were not wounded. Acuña asked him, "Why didn't you surrender sooner?" And the other answered, "We've been hollering surrender for the last hour but you were firing so much that you didn't hear us." That was the truth.

PONCE: We were camping at Alegría del Pío—it was just after the landing.

UNIVERSO: December fifth at four in the afternoon.

AMEJEIRAS: At a little after two o'clock.

ALMEIDA: No, it was four-thirty in the afternoon. I know because I looked at my watch. Ramirito was passing out crackers and sausage.

AMEJEIRAS: That's right, with sausage. I ate some.

ALMEIDA: Ramirito had said, "I can't pass them out before four."

UNIVERSO: Yes. At four the planes came by. And at four forty-five we were attacked. My meal got left behind.

AMEJEIRAS: My boots, too.

UNIVERSO: Mine, too.

PONCE: Everybody had gotten himself settled. Then there was the first shot, fired by the officer commanding the soldiers.

AMEJEIRAS: Nobody heard that shot—

PONCE: Some people heard it. Then there was a whole barrage. Terrible. We crawled along the ground. I realized I was wounded and tried to drag myself into a field of sugar cane. But I couldn't because the gunfire was so thick. I pulled back and I heard someone crying, "We're beaten. We'd better give up!" Then Almeida's voice, "Nobody surrenders, goddam it!"

AMEJEIRAS: He said worse. . . .

PONCE: Right. Censored. We dispersed. I beat a retreat and by a little path I began shooting my Johnson, blindly, in the direction of their fire. You remember, Almeida? I was beside you. I told you, "Almeida, I'm beat."

ALMEIDA: And I said, "Me too, Ponce, I can't do any more."

PONCE: We were side by side, shooting.

ALMEIDA: I said, "We'll crawl over there." It was a big tree trunk. Crawling toward it, we were joined by Pino, the two Fuenteses and Che, who was wounded.

PONCE: Then I said to Almeida, "I can't go on. Leave me in the field."

ALMEIDA: Just then Alventosa came along.

PONCE: He had a bullet in his throat. Soon it was Raulito Suárez' turn with a hand barely dangling from his arm. That's when we asked Faustino to pass his handkerchief along to the wounded comrade.

AMEJEIRAS: When they set the cane field on fire it was like being in hell.

PONCE: I spent two days out in those fields dying of thirst. I was drinking my urine. One day I lost consciousness.

They dropped napalm bombs on us. I escaped them because when the flames reached me (I still have the scars from it) I leaped away. I could not get up. Later the doctor told me it was on account of an internal hemorrhage. By chance I had jumped into a clearing around a large stake that had been cut down at ground level. And I stayed there.

I could hear the guards, then I fell unconscious. Time passed, I came to and tried crawling away and couldn't make it. Then I remember taking my belt, having lost all hope, and tying it to a bush (stupid thing to do) so I could hang myself. A little bush, almost flattened out. I couldn't do anything more. It was awful. A moment came when I resigned myself, thinking, "So, this is the end. . . ."

AMEJEIRAS: Where did the bullet hit you?

PONCE: Here, in the chest. Yes, I stayed in that one spot. I heard roosters crowing—

AMEJEIRAS: This Ponce is impossible. No matter where you take him the first bullet has his name on it. It's no use, he doesn't know how to kill, just how to get killed!

PONCE: Well, I heard some roosters crowing and told myself, "There must be a house close by. Let's see if I can make it." I tried but I couldn't walk, so I crawled along, making some progress. I figured, "It isn't far from Pilón. If I make it to that house nearby I'll tell them to get in touch with Celia Sánchez for me."

But the shells which hadn't exploded before now were going off because of the fire, and the guards started searching around. At first they didn't see me behind the pole, covered with dirt and ashes. . . . The next thing, I woke up in prison at Moncada. I don't remember anything else.

AMEJEIRAS: I was with Raul and Ciro. Altogether there were six of us in our group, but there were only

five when we reached Fidel. That was on December
17. Almeida and his comrades had arrived two days
earlier. It was a moving reunion.

UNIVERSO: It was the first contact Fidel had with
any group since the Alegría del Pío disaster. Fidel
couldn't believe it when they told him a group of his
people were at Hermes Caldero's farm. Now he is a
major in the army, but then was only a peasant comrade. Fidel feared a trap.

"You're not telling me anything concrete," he told
his informant. "How are they?"

"Very well—"

"How are they dressed?"

"They've got uniforms like yours."

"And their weapons?"

"Well, there's one with a Thompson, another with
a rifle, another with a Johnson."

"Good. Let them send me something I can identify
them by."

Raul sent him his Mexican driver's license along
with a message and Fidel saw it was true, no trap
at all, and that night he sent for us. We met in a
canefield. Fidel embraced us. He was so happy to see
us! He told us that we shouldn't despair, that it was
only the beginning, that our first defeat was a valuable experience and that we must get used to guerilla
life and never drop our guard. Afterwards, Almeida
came with the others.

UNIVERSO: After the battle I stayed with Fidel,
only with him. At nightfall Faustino joined us and
we began the long march to Mongo Pérez' place. That

lasted seven or eight days. We were waiting for Crescencio, the guide. We had heard there were lots of Rebels in the Sierra. It was true.

AMEJEIRAS: Those groups joined up with the peasants Crescencio had organized. They all came there because they were looking for us somewhere in those mountains. We others found Fidel in more haphazard fashion with no guides, just by pushing ahead day and night.

UNIVERSO: Fidel made a beautiful speech. He said, "We have already won the war." He was very moved and he spoke very well because we had shaped up as a first-rate team. There had been more than eighty of us working together in Mexico and crossing in the *Granma.* Now there were only twelve of us left.

Chapter Two

UNIVERSO

I'm going to tell you what Fidel, Faustino and I did on December 5, 1956, after three days of marching. We were taking a little break at Alegría del Pío. It must have been a quarter past four in the afternoon when the planes appeared. More than ten of them, different kinds: B-26s, observation planes, and others. We didn't pay much attention because we figured they couldn't spot us.

As I said, at a quarter past four we were resting under the trees in a spot that wasn't very well-chosen. Nowadays we wouldn't make the mistake of taking cover in a place like that.

We heard a shot. I believe it was Comrade Ramiro who gave the alarm, "Soldiers!" At that moment a barrage broke out. A real hail of bullets. The soldiers, taking advantage of the aircrafts' noise, had approached without our noticing. Now they were very near and shouting at us. Our sleeping comrades woke up and began firing back. Our column was thrown into total confusion. The soldiers were so close our people no longer knew where their own comrades were.

I remember Comrade Juan Almeida crying out when they told us to give ourselves up: "Nobody surrenders!" Almeida kept repeating that, "Nobody surrenders!" and went on firing.

I was part of a group of non-coms under Raul Castro's direction. There was Ciro Redondo, Julio Díaz and some others. We were to be commanding troop units when enough men had been recruited by us. That was to be our eventual responsibility.

In this confusion the comrades started falling back toward a plantation which had been set afire by incendiary bombs. I had sores on my feet. I had taken off my boots, knapsack and bandolier. When the attack broke, I swept up everything—bandolier, rifle, shoes, pack and a box of cartridges. Because of all that stuff I was falling behind the others in our retreat. In this kind of war one shouldn't make mistakes like that. I never did it again in the Sierra Maestra. In the Sierra I spent several months without taking off my boots, not even to sleep. They became part of my body.

As I fell back toward the canefield, I found Fidel.

He was giving orders. He was moving about all by himself so I stayed with him. I passed his instructions on to every comrade who came by. Meanwhile, the rifle fire got worse and Juan Manuel Márquez joined us. He told Fidel, "Our comrades are pulling back. It's better not to fire from here. Let's get out, we're too close."

Soldiers were about a hundred yards from us. The hail of bullets went on, digging in the dirt around us. They had the high ground, while we could see nothing. We were in the middle of the canefield but the cane shoots were still too small, hardly chest high. The soldiers spotted us suddenly and then it really rained on us.

Juan Manuel Márquez convinced Fidel that we ought to fall back with the others. We began to move toward a small woods, going on a line parallel to that of the soldiers. Fidel would run six or seven yards, then it was Juan Manuel's turn, then it was mine. We rotated like that. But then Juan Manuel did not catch up to us and Fidel sent me back to look for him. Crawling back, I came to the place where I'd seen him last, I called him a few times but couldn't find him.

We continued falling back but, once closer to our objective, had to wait until dark to get from the canefield into the woods, because there was an open area between them and soldiers would have spotted us crossing it.

Toward six o'clock, as evening fell, I saw someone coming—I thought it was a soldier. I warned Fidel as he approached. We were in a little grove of the plantation. Fidel said, "Fire at him if he gets closer." But when this guy came nearer I saw from his dress and boots that he was one of us. I called to him and he came over. I recognized Faustino Pérez. He told us about the dead comrades, about the wounded. At nightfall we made it to the woods.

Juan Manuel Márquez was murdered later in another place. I don't know how it happened, but they captured him, then killed him. He must have gone off in some other direction. But he hadn't been wounded because when I looked for him I didn't see any trace of blood. We had run more than thirty yards, throwing ourselves flat on our stomachs, over and over again. He couldn't have been wounded then—we would have found some traces of him.

As soon as day broke, I went back with Fidel and Faustino to the plantation. Fidel was worried about the rest of our comrades. His one thought was to regroup them.

I had mounted guard all night while Fidel and Faustino got some rest. As I've said, we were a little disoriented so we decided to stay out in the canefield and try to join up with our comrades. The wooded area wasn't very big and, if we stayed there now, getting out later might mean crossing the open ground when soldiers were on the lookout in greater numbers.

But the plants in the field were too small, almost like shoots, and a pilot caught sight of us under a thicket. The plane flew very low over us and Fidel said we'd have to get out of there. We did; and, right after, a B-26 machine-gunned the thicket. We continued pushing on in leaps and rushes until we found tall enough shoots of cane and were no longer visible.

We began talking about our comrades. Fidel's one thought was to get out of there and, no matter what the cost, to regroup the men. Faustino and I persuaded him to stay put because our comrades had fallen back to God knew where. And after all, if there was anyone to be worried about, it was the man who was directing the Revolution and was going to depose Batista. He oughtn't take any chance of falling into enemy hands. That's the way I put it.

We asked Faustino how long we could hold out on sugar cane. Several days, he answered, like a doctor giving advice. So we decided to hole up there while the enemy surrounded us. I think we went three days without drinking anything. Each morning we would lick the damp cane leaves to ease the night's thirst.

At the end of three or more days (I can't remember whether it was three or five days) we began advancing across the plantation. Soldiers passed close by. At night we heard the rattle of submachine guns as our comrades moved about looking for water. We marched like that a few days without meeting anybody, without seeing a house. I remember how once we passed through a little place called Río Frío. There were soldiers all over. The houses were full of them but we passed right by without anyone noticing us. We were taking all precautions, always on the alert and finger on the trigger.

We finally came to a peasant's house. But before

that we had come to a little farm and I had looked around for something to eat. I found two small pumpkins, and we cooked some ears of corn and bananas. We roasted the corn in a ditch. The weight of our weapons, plus the dry food, naturally got us thirstier. We were exhausted after so many days without nourishment. On the *Granma*, during the crossing from Mexico, our food had consisted of pills which, they told us, had the food values of a chicken or beefsteak. I even had taken cod liver oil a few times.

Well, we arrived at nightfall before this farmhouse. We were soaking wet, protecting our rifles from the water. We first had to see what was happening there on account of the soldiers. With the telescopic sight we saw everything. We also learned the names of their little girl, their dog, and so on. Toward six in the evening Fidel gave orders to Faustino to go to the house. As soon as Faustino got there, he signaled us and we came forward. We told the peasant that we were twenty-five Rebels and that we wished to eat. Immediately, we took security measures. Fidel ordered a watch to be kept on the house; nobody was to go out while we were in there. We managed it without having to mistreat those good people.

We slaughtered a pig for twenty-five people (we said our comrades would be coming along later). The woman of the house, happy to see us, kept saying, "You poor men! How hungry you must be! Near here there are Batista troops. I'll show you where myself." And she showed us a safe-conduct card dropped from a plane. She also told us that the loudspeaker of a cub plane, flying low, had kept calling for the men to surrender. We learned the latest news and saw some government leaflets.

The meal over, we asked about several roads. As to the food for our twenty-two other comrades, we took it along in a sack to eat en route.

We reached Limones. At this place there's a hamlet and a small woods, but we decided to hide in the high grass where it would be hard for anyone to find us. My peasant experience had taught me that. A few minutes later buzzards started wheeling overhead. Fidel said, "Those birds got the habit from eating our dead comrades." I began waving to drive them away; they could make things seem suspicious in our area and attract attention to us.

I saw a peasant who was holding something in his hands, looking around. Fidel ordered me to bring him over. I crept about a hundred yards through the grass and reached the road. "Halt!"I shouted at the peasant, pointing my rifle at him, then I signaled for him to come into the bushes. There he told me he was bringing us some food. I looked into the container he was holding and inside there was yellow rice with turkey, also bread, coffee and milk. I led him over to Fidel, since this was obviously a decent guy. Fidel got into a friendly talk with him.

I remember Fidel was wearing a major's star on his cap. The peasant began telling stories of the War of Independence. He told us that one day the Spaniards killed one of General Maceo's officers and were able to identify him because of the star he was wearing.

Then he exclaimed, looking at Fidel, "You have the air of a commander, of a chief!" The matter rested there but we had the feeling that he had recognized Fidel and we didn't like it. Fidel hadn't said who he was.

Fidel asked the peasant for a little oil to clean our rifles, which were rusty from the rain. Later the peasant sent a small boy with a bottle. As soon as he got to us, the kid said, "Which one is Fidel? My father sends him this oil." Hearing that, we became still more uneasy. We got away from there soon afterwards. Actually, that was a mistake because we later learned this peasant was the father of Guillermo García, a great revolutionary. He could have given us plenty of help, since having lost our bearings and contact with everybody, we didn't even know where we were.

The kid who brought the oil was Guillermo García's brother. When he asked for Fidel, we looked all around and then I told him to give the oil to "Alejandro" (which was Fidel's pseudonym in the Sierra).

Shortly after this incident we took off and hid ourselves even more thoroughly. After some days Guillermo García (now a major in the Rebel Army) joined us. He told us numerous combat episodes after Alegría del Pío and repeated for our benefit the rumors going around. He also told us which comrades were dead. He brought five rifles abandoned in the field. Finally, he spoke about Crescencio, who was giving us his support and was now in the Sierra. That was when Fidel gave the order to start for the Sierra Maestra.

We took the road looking for Mongo Pérez, Crescencio's brother and a good revolutionary, too. At that time the group consisted of Fidel, Faustino, our guides and myself. Mongo gave us plenty of help. He hid us in a field of sugarcane. We slept and ate at his place without anybody suspecting our presence. We sent somebody with news to Crescencio, who at that time was busy with lots of things, helping out comrades and hiding them. We began to find out that our men were scattered all over; one of them was wounded in the neck, "a man suffering from asthma." We realized that was Che.

Fidel sent for our comrades and they came in groups. We saw them arrive in the following days; Raul, Che, Almeida, Julio Díaz, Ciro Redondo, Camilo, Calixto García, Almejeiras, Luís Crespo, each with a rifle, although almost out of ammunition. Elated, Fidel exclaimed, "We'll win this war! We are just beginning to fight!"

It was a few days before Christmas. The father-in-law of Mongo Pérez, a very good-hearted peasant, cooked two suckling pigs and we celebrated the oncoming victory of the Revolution.

Chapter Three

CELIA SÁNCHEZ AND HAYDÉE SANTAMARÍA

—Let's begin with Frank.

CELIA: When I saw him for the first time—or rather when I met him—that was after Fidel came out of prison and I took Pedrito Miret to my house in Pilón.

HAYDEE: I remember seeing Frank the first time at a meeting of the National Directorate of the 26th of July Movement. He had been sent to take over his Santiago assignment. He used to tell me, "If you wouldn't think so much about those who are dead you'd make a wonderful revolutionary." When Jossué fell he wrote a letter in which he said, "Yeyé, for the first time I understand what you've had to go through, and your feelings. Forgive me."

After Frank's death I received a letter he wrote only a few days before, telling me the police were on his trail and that all he asked for was thirty more days of life "to put the finishing touches to my task."

CELIA: Before Frank came to my place in Pilón, I had seen him with Pepito Tey at a Manzanillo meeting, after Fidel left the Isle of Pines, when the 26th of July Movement was organized. He came to Pilón with Pedrito Miret because we were studying the expedition's landing problem and we wanted to inspect the coastal area to get a better idea of water depths. I had the depth readings in our Pilón office; one day I asked for those maps with all the indications to be sent to me, but I never received them. I recall that afterwards they found them on the *Granma* and brought them to Papa, wrapped in a woman's blouse to make him think I had sneaked on board with the others—

—You had a plan to await Fidel's arrival in Cuba?

CELIA: Yes, and also to get him weapons. They had decided that Echevarría, who knew the coast, could be the guide from El Pilón or El Macho or La Magdalena. That area would have been perfect for the landing. If they arrived there, we could bring arms from Pilón or Niquero in trucks and cars.

From the 29th on we had transport vehicles and fuel supplies in all these places. Groups were gathered at Manzanillo and Campechuela. We had people all over who knew the country well.

We were also in contact with Crescencio's family and with the Acuñas, in case the landing took place near them. We also had Carracedo, who was called El Jabao, and also Crescencio's son, Ignacio, later killed at the Battle of Jiguaní, who was a truckdriver for the sugar mill.

We sent the Campechuela people out in the bush to get ready. Without arms, because we only had two M-1 rifles.

—Where were you the day of the landing?

CELIA: We were in the Sierra. The morning of the 29th we arrived at Crescencio's place. We spent the 30th there, waiting. As soon as I got there, I told Crescencio, "You'd better get going, compañero. Fidel is coming and you must wait for him with all your men, without telling anybody." Crescencio, who is the calmest man I know, said, "One moment." He went into his room, and a few minutes later came out all dressed in white. With his street shoes, a jacket, a tie and a felt hat, as if we weren't way out in the country but in the middle of a city party. And his revolver in his belt. At Niquero, Fajardo and his men were hiding in the freezing room of an ice plant which, fortunately, was not in use.

—When did you learn of the landing?

CELIA: Right away, because of what was happening. Batista's planes began bombing the Niquero area. The army blocked all roads. Only soldiers could move about freely. We had to bury ourselves up in the Sierra to try to make contact with Fidel. When we couldn't establish contact I decided to go back down. Ignacio was to go to Pilón.

—You were far from the point of debarkment?

CELIA: Well, since it wasn't raining, the roads weren't bad, so it took an hour to reach Niquero, then another quarter of an hour to the landing place. We had sent some men along the telephone line to cut the circuit between Niquero and Pilón so the army would be without communications. That way one group from the *Granma* could attack Niquero, another Pilón. At Pilón they would already be in the Sierra. There wouldn't be any problem. But unhappily, when it came to carrying out the plans. . . .

Just consider where the landing took place. If they had debarked right on the beach instead of at the swamp, they would have found trucks, jeeps, gasoline. It would have been a walkaway. And the barracks was closer by. A real surprise attack and a well-armed one would have been possible.

As for me, all the guards knew me and I could drive everywhere without their asking questions.

You, Haydée, were you at Santiago?

HAYDEE: Yes, I was at Rodríguez Font's home in Santiago.

—When did you first meet Fidel?

HAYDEE: A little after March 10, 1952, at my place. Abel, my brother, brought him over. I remember I'd just swept the floor and he was dropping ashes all over, and he never stopped pacing up and down. When he left I asked Abel, "Who is this person who was messing up everything?" He told me all about him.

I remember that before the landing Celia wanted to go to Mexico to make the trip back with Fidel, and how Frank came to Havana to stop her. We didn't know her well yet.

CELIA: Some people were saying I ought to leave Cuba, it was dangerous for me to stay because I was too well known. But Frank was against that, it wasn't his idea. I went to Havana to see him. I discussed it with Yeyé and she said I had to decide for myself. But I was determined above all to be present at the great day, and I kept wondering, "Suppose you go to Mexico and then they don't let you come back with them?"

HAYDEE: I had the same fear. Frank said about Celia, "I'm terribly afraid my stopping her from going may bring her trouble, but she's more useful here. She knows her part of the country so well." Frank wasn't a man to talk offhandedly and he said her presence in Cuba was of decisive importance.

CELIA: Well, I finally chose to stay.

HAYDEE: Now I know that if I had come on the *Granma* I'd be dead today .

CELIA: And it would have been one more trouble for Fidel and the others, worrying about a woman.

HAYDEE: But I didn't stop dreaming that they would let me come back with them from Mexico. Later on, in the Sierra, my dream was to come down from the mountains with Fidel. When we were climbing and I couldn't go on, when Celia was the only woman still climbing, Fidel would say to me, "Taking a rest?" I'd answer "no," but I really was exhausted.

My consolation was in telling myself: "Now I'm climbing, but one day I'll be descending these mountains to Santiago." That hope sustained me when Enrique died and Armando was captured. And yet, when they did come down to Santiago, I was far away in Miami!

—You were more useful to the Revolution in Miami.

HAYDEE: Yes, at least we were sending money.

CELIA: They had money, a plane, weapons and equipment.

HAYDEE: Returning to Santiago was a matter to be settled between our dead and us. I never go to cemeteries, but I told myself, "When I get to Santiago with my comrades they will go to the military post, but I will go to the cemetery and tell our dead: Look, we have arrived." That helped keep me marching.

When Fidel told me I had to go to Miami! If Raul,

Che or Armando himself had said it, I wouldn't have gone. But it was a difficult time and Fidel said, "Let's see if you can do the job." So I went. That was shortly after the failure of the April strike.

—The atmosphere at Miami was stifling.

HAYDEE: It wasn't merely a question of collecting money, but of contacting all the groups. Two months after my arrival we could say for the first time that the Movement was organized over there. And not only in Miami, but also in the whole U. S. A. Each month we collected twelve to fifteen thousand dollars, one peseta after the other, one centavo after the other. From California, from New York. . . .

And there were other problems. Like those we had with Díaz Lanz and with Lorié. Once I gave Lorié five hundred dollars for a trip. He took off to Venezuela and sent his wife I don't know where with ten thousand dollars. I kept all that to myself because I figured at least some of it would reach the Sierra. But when the messengers with my letters reached Raul or Fidel they told them everything and my letters couldn't hide anything from them.

—And Moncada, Haydée, the attack?

HAYDEE: Melba Hernández remembers it best. I can't recall the exact details. But if I start talking about Moncada many things are bound to come back to me.

Now that I think about the people who attacked

Moncada and about Fidel himself, I wonder how it's possible that Fidel, being as he is, ended up with anybody betraying him. How is it possible that we didn't all perfectly identify ourselves with him, with the Revolution?

Each time that I see Fidel, that I talk to him or see him on television, I think about the others, all those who died and those who are living, and I think of Fidel, the Fidel that we know, that Fidel who is still the same as ever.

Well, we were in the Siboney house—Melba, Abel, Renato, Elpidio and me. Renato had the idea of making a *chilindrón* of chicken. When he began explaining it to me I laughed and showed him it wasn't a *chilindrón* but a fricassee. Renato told me, "Nope, that's what they call it in Vuelta Abajo country."

While cooking and discussing things with Melba and Renato, I kept looking at my brother Abel and remembering the last time we went to say goodbye to the family. When we were leaving the house to return to Havana, Aida told us to make sure we didn't wake up the little girl. Abel wanted to take her in his arms. I said to Aida, "Let us do it. This may be the last time we see her." Aida looked at me, frightened, and I tried to joke, "Sure, we might have an accident on the road." "Don't be so dramatic!" Aida answered.

When Renato's *chilindrón* was ready, Abel didn't want to eat. He went to Santiago with a couple of old friends who lived nearby. I thought, "Maybe this is the last carnival they'll ever go to."

Melba was with me; for seven months we hadn't

been apart as much as one day. I thought about the house, about Melba who was beside me, about our comrades. At that time I wasn't thinking about death. Two things were on my mind: the first was that when all was finished, if Fidel was still there making the Revolution, our lives and our deeds would have a meaning. The other came later, the anguish we felt when we first understood that we would never again see our dead, fallen in their blood on the dust. Then I was afraid of leaving Melba.

I had come to Moncada with those I loved most. There were Abel and Boris, Melba, Fidel and Renato and Elpidio and Raul, the poet, Mario, Chenard and the others. And there was Cuba. At stake were our starved people, their freedom violated, and the Revolution which would fulfill their destiny.

Our comrades were hungry. When midnight came we were busy chatting and laughing. We joked and kidded around. Coffee was made and we ate the remains of the dinner, what Abel had refused. We exchanged anecdotes. Like the time I was traveling to Santiago with two valises filled with arms, so heavy that a soldier on the train who bumped into them asked me if I were transporting dynamite. "No," I told him, "books. I've just finished my exams. I hope to relax a little at the carnival. You'd be nice company there." The soldier gave me a friendly smile and asked where we should meet. When I got off the train he helped me with the valises. Abel and Renato were waiting in the station. "I'd like to introduce you to a travel acquaintance," I said. Then I told the soldier,

"These two friends have been waiting for me." The soldier turned over the valises and we left him. A comrade ribbed Boris about it: "Keep an eye on Yeyé —she has a date with a soldier of the regime—" That got a good laugh.

Fidel arrived first, then everybody else. Some singly, some in groups. Afterwards, on the trip to Moncada, I thought about the next day. What was going to happen? What would they say at home?

At last we got there.

After that came the first seconds, then the hours. The worst, the bloodiest and most violent of our lives. Hours in which there was nothing but heroism, when everything was sacred. Life and death can be noble and beautiful when you fight for your life but give it up without compromise.

What happened Melba remembers very well and I have tried in vain to forget completely. I recall the time through a haze of smoke and anguish. Fidel tells it in his book, *History Will Absolve Me.* The death of Boris, of Abel. That death which wrenched so many comrades from us and stained walls and grass with their blood.

There are moments when nothing inspires fear, neither pain, nor machine gun outbursts, nor smoke, nor the smell of burnt flesh, nor the feeling of warm blood.

There is the moment when all can be beautiful, heroic. The moment when life defies death and defeat because one holds on to it and because it is important not to lose it. And at such a moment one can risk all to preserve what really counts. That passion which led us to attack Moncada bears the names of Abel, Renato, Mario and so many others, but in the highest moments it can spell Cuba itself.

A man was approaching. We heard a new outburst of machine gun fire. I ran to the window. Melba followed me. I felt her hands on my shoulders. I saw the man coming closer and did not hear the voice saying, "They have killed your brother!" I felt Melba's hands still there. I heard myself saying without recognizing my own voice, "Abel?" The man did not answer. Melba came still closer. All of her was in those hands holding me. "What time is it?" I asked. Melba answered, "Nine o'clock."

There are the facts which have stayed in my memory. I remember nothing else, but from that moment on I thought of no one except Fidel. We were all thinking of him. Of Fidel who could not die, who must stay alive to carry on the Revolution, of Fidel's life which was the life of all of us. From the moment that we knew Fidel was still alive, Abel and Boris and Renato and the others were not dead to us.

CELIA: People who know Fidel from before really understand what he is like. Those who now see the Camilo Cienfuegos School, the armed militia—Fidel was already speaking of those things in the Sierra when we had nothing to eat! "A great school for twenty thousand children. We will do many things; educate, prepare the people; but we will have to continue arming ourselves. . . ." And I thought, "Arm ourselves? For what? When we've won we won't need arms any more!" Even up there it wasn't so easy to get the peasants to use weapons despite the way they had been oppressed. Fidel had to talk to them endlessly. Yes, Fidel saw everything clearly.

Fidel spoke of those things up in the mountains and now you see them all being realized. The people's stores, as he organized them in the Sierra at the time when speculation made it necessary to get rid of middlemen. He foresaw everything.

—And Matthews, the American journalist, he went

with you up into the Sierra?

CELIA: No, that was some days later.

HAYDEE: The whole group arrived together and we slept in the same house. Celia left several hours before us. She went with Frank.

CELIA: Yes. We marched all night with Frank, and at five in the morning we met Fidel. On the way Frank, Echeverría and I found Luís Crespo, who had become lost after a skirmish.

HAYDEE: You left for the camp with Frank while Vilma and I left at five in the morning. Then it was Faustino's turn and another man's. We got lost and had to sleep out in the open.

CELIA: In the morning, when we got to camp, we fixed the place up so that Matthews would get a good impression. We were also to make him think there was another camp and that Fidel was there. Raul kept passing back and forth with the same men.

Later on, came Bob Taber and other American journalists. That was after we had established the camp in the woods near Manzanillo.

HAYDEE: But a lot more went on during Bob Taber's trip. I remember we were hiding in a coffee plantation at Lalo Sardiñas' place and there were soldiers about. Fidel learned the spot we were in and sent Camilo with his group to help us. "Save them, no matter what the cost!" he ordered them.

—When did you girls get to know each other?

CELIA: In Havana. At Melba Hernández' home. Do you remember? After the big meeting I came to see you and Pedrito Miret. We talked all night; you were then engaged to Armando. It wasn't long before your marriage.

Once I was waiting for them in a park. I didn't know they were engaged. I saw them with their arms about each other and I thought, "That's a funny way to plot!" A very pleasant way!

HAYDEE: Yes, but we certainly must have been talking about the Revolution then.

—February was the first time you went to see Fidel in the Sierra?

CELIA: Yes, the first time.

HAYDEE: I remember one time when Frank was cleaning a gun. He said to me, "Yeyé, we have to find a way to get Fidel out of Cuba. He has to get to a Latin American country where he can reorganize the Movement. I've never spoken to him about it, but we have to find a way to tell him. He could get himself killed here and we can't afford to lose him."

When we saw Fidel we started staring at each other without knowing how to begin. But Fidel said, "The soldiers are busy in the lowlands, but they don't dare come up here. If you get me enough rifles and ammunition I promise you that in two months I'll give them a real fight." Neither Frank nor I had the heart to say anything more. He had such conviction! And don't think he was asking for a lot: only twenty rifles and ammunition.

CELIA: Frank left thoroughly convinced. Now he saw things as Fidel did. And at that time there were only eighteen partisans in the Sierra Maestra!

That night we went looking for a small house we had spotted during the day. There were Fidel, Armando, Frank, Vilma and me; and Luís Crespo, always a loner, who offered to be our guide. We didn't find the house. But we had gone so far that we couldn't get back to the road in time, so we slept under the stars. That same morning Matthews arrived in camp. Universo brought us the news. He was instructed to go back and tell the journalist to wait there for Fidel who was coming from another camp.

—And the first camp at Manzanillo?

CELIA: We established it to recruit troops at Manzanillo and to send men and arms from there to Fidel. It was on a small rice farm, not far from the prison.

There, in a coffee plantation, we set up camp. No one would suppose that there was a camp in that treeless area. We had some people there, and more came from Santiago. That was the first Manzanillo group.

HAYDEE: There were no weapons for them then.

CELIA: We learned that Bob Taber was going to come up with other American journalists. Haydée accompanied Armando to Havana to make the arrangements. That was in March.

HAYDEE: Right. That was when Armando was captured at Virgen del Camino. I managed to escape, scurrying away like a street urchin. I had a lot of money on me, I was terribly afraid they'd get the money we collected. A policeman chased me, but I zigzagged away between some autos.

CELIA: We stayed at Bayamo to arrange things. Nicaragua and I were hiding out with a family of frightened souls. Escalona brought us the news of Armando's capture but no one knew anything about Yeyé or the American newspapermen.

However, Escalona had parked his station wagon on the wrong side of the street and the police came around looking for the owner. Just as Guerrita came out, a bomb went off nearby and the police began searching all the houses, revolvers drawn. Nicaragua and I jumped over the wall back of the place where we were staying. We hid for a while, and then, at six o'clock, Haydée arrived with the Americans.

HAYDEE: When I got in Bayamo I couldn't figure out where to go because nobody was in the houses I knew. I began driving the car around, telling my

Americans I was trying to signal the comrades.

CELIA: Guerrita had been arrested and he was the only one who knew how to contact Haydée. When the police left, we went back to the house. The people there told us to get out and we said we wouldn't. They had taken my bed apart but I went to lie down in the little girl's bed. Nicaragua stayed up to keep an eye on them so they wouldn't go and denounce us. They woke me at six in the morning but I told them it was too soon to leave. "Haven't you any coffee?" I asked. The woman hadn't prepared any.

HAYDEE: We kept driving around and around. . . . Then I remembered a dentist I knew and I told Marcello to let me off there, make three turns around the block and come back. I saw the dentist, he didn't want to have anything to do with it, but all the same, we left the Americans with him and then went back to Manzanillo.

CELIA: Finally, all of us, including the Americans and Yeyé, got together at Vallejo's place. During the night we took a jeep with Lalo Sardiñas driving. On the road he met Rafael Castro. Lalo told us, "Go to my place, I'll be waiting for you." We didn't know what to say because I had an idea he was working with the soldiers. Well, we did go there and then we heard soldiers approaching. We hid in his coffee grove, thinking he had sold us out.

The military came and we couldn't leave the place we were hiding in. Fidel learned about it and, as Yeyé said, gave Camilo orders to get us out "no matter what the cost." That was in March, shortly after the attack on the presidential palace.

HAYDEE: When Camilo's men came we thought they were soldiers.

CELIA: If any soldiers had so much as entered that grove they would have seen us.

Well, when we got back to camp at long last, we learned that Rafael Castro was there and had brought along a submachine gun. It turned out Lalo and Rafael had known each other all along and yet neither had said a word about it, a word that would have erased all suspicion about him.

HAYDEE: In that coffee grove our fate was completely in Lalo's hands.

CELIA: It was Saturday before Easter. People were dancing in all the houses. Each time a dog barked, Lalo worried that we would be discovered.

HAYDEE: And the Americans—they could hardly go on—

CELIA: From there we went up Turquino peak. It was the first time any of us had climbed the Turquino, even Fidel.

HAYDEE: When I took off my shoes, my feet were covered with blood.

CELIA: She had enormous sores. She always looked for new sandals. They were better for her but had to be washed all the time and dried by the fire. Each day she used up a pair.

HAYDEE: But Celia just marched on and on and on—I told myself, "After all, I'm like her. I'll do whatever she'll do!"

CELIA: Yes, but you did have your asthma and those feet to contend with.

—And your first battle, Celia?

CELIA: That was at El Uvero. Before that they had killed Domínguez on a road. He went ahead of his squad and came to the road where the police waited. They took him by surprise and killed him. That was the day Haydée arrived.

HAYDEE: Fidel didn't want to take us to the attack on San Ramon.

CELIA: That was the first battle we saw, both of us together.

HAYDEE: We were then at La Habanita; we kept telling each other that he wouldn't let us come along. Celia said, "Well, they have another thought coming!" Then Fidel did tell us, "You girls wait for us at—" I don't remember the name of the place.

CELIA: We told him to go with everybody else. There was *no* reason for leaving us behind. So we got to go. Vilma also was there, her feet soaked with blood.

HAYDEE: We believed Horacio Rodríguez was dead because he had been wounded during the attack. Some peasants told us he had been killed. We went to bury him but found him alive. Doctor Vallejo operated on him in a cabin by flashlight. He had several stomach perforations.

San Ramón was the first time we used mortars and a .50-calibre machine gun.

CELIA: It was in June, 1958. Our plane had come a few days before with the machine gun.

—At what time did the fighting begin?

HAYDEE: About two in the morning.

CELIA: The military post was in the middle of the village and we had to be very careful. For us it was mainly a show of force. Not a question of taking the post, but of showing we had mortars and a machine gun and could use them.

HAYDEE: After San Ramón we captured some wounded soldiers, as did Angelito Verdecia in another attack.

We had lost all notion of time. Night passed, came daytime, and still mines kept exploding.

CELIA: Grenades went off in a truck, killing many soldiers. The planes were bombing the area. At five in the morning the next day, Fidel, Haydée and I went into a house at Las Vegas de Jibacoa. We were dog-tired. Just when we were going to sleep we received a message from Che. Fidel said, "Read it. If it's important, let me see it. If not, I'll look at it later on." And he stretched out to sleep. It wasn't important, so I held on to it. Then we all fell asleep.

At ten in the morning the planes started bombing the house.

HAYDEE: We woke up. Celia told me to take our detonators and get out with Fidel while she looked around for that message from Che. Fidel went out and I followed him on the run.

There was a large rock nearby and Fidel told me to hide behind it but I wanted him to use it himself. A plane spotted us and began firing. We both ducked behind that rock. The plane kept firing but Celia did not come.

Each time the plane made a pass I called Celia. You know what was the matter? She had fallen asleep again and had heard nothing! She didn't even wake up when the plane started aiming directly for the house again.

CELIA: When I woke up, I saw nobody was in the house. I couldn't remember a thing.

HAYDEE: I think she was half asleep while she talked to us when we went out. After that adventure, when I was back in the plains, the sight of a plane always made me wonder whether our comrades up in the Sierra weren't being bombed. I don't think anything was as hard for us as that experience, not even Moncada.

At Moncada I suffered so much that for a while I became numb to it all. Abel was dead, Boris was dead, and I did not even cry. I was feeling nothing, was I suffering? Before seeing Fidel, I felt I had died. We were unprepared for so much horror.

—July 26 I arrived in Santiago with Ferrer, the photographer. That day and the next we tried to join you but couldn't.

HAYDEE: Panchito Cano saw us at Moncada during the day. When we saw him we all had the same impression, "That man's not a cop or a shifty character."

He photographed us.

—It was a good idea on Fidel's part, getting to the mountains.

CELIA: He had always said we should.

HAYDEE: Boris had returned to Siboney where he found Ramirito Valdés. Ramirito told him he had no news of us and so returned to Santiago. That's when Boris got caught. He had already reached the mountain highway but turned around.

My brother Abel had a pleasant, optimistic nature —so much so that I never believed anything bad could happen to him. At Siboney, that evening before the attack, he didn't stop joking. He told us, "Fidel's going to give a really big surprise to the Cubans. It'll give me a great kick!" (Of course, he wasn't referring to that one attack, but to the Revolution itself.)

But, I was sure Boris would be killed. He felt it, too. He told me, "Do you realize what it is to die for such a cause? Not everybody has that chance. The one thing that bothers me is my mother. Because—well, you're young, you can continue to struggle, but what is there for an old woman?" That's why I take such good care of his mother. It was a constant concern for him.

—Camilo also gave the impression he never thought about death, but I think he had a premonition he would die young.

CELIA: A week before he died we went to Ciénaga

de Zapata. Fidel was in the dining-room telling about things that had happened in the Sierra. Camilo was stretched out and I was reading. At some point in the conversation Camilo said, "Ah yes—in a few years you'll still hear Fidel telling those stories, but everybody will be old then and he'll say, 'You remember Camilo? He died just about when it was all over.'" He said *that* a week before his end!

Paz also was really brave and Fidel had great confidence in him. Never spoke of dying. The day he was killed he had begun a letter to his children in which he said goodbye to them and told them to keep fighting behind Fidel. He didn't even have time to sign it.

HAYDEE: Not a long time ago I said in an interview with Pablo Hernández that I thought the Moncada attack hasn't received the historical recognition it should have.

CELIA: That's because you see Moncada as we all see it, the beginning of the struggle. Moncada was the birth of the Revolution.

HAYDEE: Pablo Hernández said to me, "You speak of Moncada without sadness." I explained that, for me, Moncada was like a woman going into birth pangs: the pain makes her cry out but it redeems her.

—It was the same for the First of January. With the great joy of victory, the memory of our dead comrades came flooding back.

HAYDEE: It was on the First of January that I truly realized Abel was dead, that they were all dead. When

I saw the parade, I looked and saw nothing.

CELIA: As for me, I constantly imagine Camilo's reactions to things. For me, he is still living. The same thing is true for Vaquerito. He was busy with supplies at Las Vegas. Each time some comrades showed themselves at his window he said, seeing them with their beards and long hair, "What do you think? They are our future patriot heroes. They'll be in the history books—you'll see!"

—Haydée, what were Abel's ideological preoccupations?

HAYDEE: He was a passionate reader of Lenin and the Soviet revolutionaries. He never stopped re-reading *Capital*. When I came in late I always found him reading.

—You remember what else he liked to read?

HAYDEE: Martí, he was a fanatic for Martí. Not long ago they brought me a bust of Martí that had belonged to him. You know, what still hurts is that he died so soon. If he had died only three year later, I would be resigned to it. He died so young . . . .

Chapter Four

GUILLERMO

Celia had been going all over Pilón in her car. Those were truly revolutionary times and the car was always filled with comrades.

Like me, some of the others were warned of the impending landing just five days before it took place. The country was seething as we passed the word to our comrades that the expedition would arrive in the near future. For myself, I was convinced that there would be such a landing. . . . We had earmarked several trucks of various kinds for carrying men without the owners being any the wiser.

We expected the landing to be made at Ojo del Toro in the Niquero district. We had observers all along that coast because nobody knew the exact spot. From the 28th on they were covering every place, but most of all Ojo del Toro.

The 30th we were advised that they had reached the coast but nothing had happened. We heard nothing of a landing that day; in fact, we only received such word the morning of the 3rd. The landing actually took place at five in the morning of the 2nd but we learned about it the next day at dawn. Troops were being moved to Niquero.

We were some 30 miles away from the landing beach. On the 3rd toward noon we started organizing patrols and alerting the population, saying that anyone who saw armed Rebels should help them. Then the army tightened up so much that contact with the population was no longer possible. There was a flood of soldiers, trucks and still more trucks.

In our zone we had organized all the youth. Later on there were plenty of dead among them, like Godofredo, the little mulatto. He was a very decent, energetic fellow, a member of Lorenzo's squad. He was killed at Las Mercedes. They used to call him Godo and he was very popular in our neighborhood.

We were divided into groups covering all sides of the sectors we could reach. We tried to locate the army and determine how encircled we might be. We were going to make contact on the 5th at Alegría del Pío. But the battle began without us at four in the afternoon.

Godo got within a half-mile of our comrades and

returned to tell us they had made contact with the army and the battle was joined. We headed toward it. I have to say it—there were some men we couldn't control. They fled like rabbits.

We're talking about those who were scared, those who took off over the hill. Why hide it? Why not talk about Chao, too, who kept telling me in the Sierra Maestra that we were mixed up in a fantastically stupid thing? He said he was a fighter like us, but that there weren't enough of us and we could never beat Batista. . . . . Why hide the truth?

And the one who cried, saying he was a school teacher, that his wife was comfortably settled in Mexico. "Why am *I* here?" he wept right in front of me.

Well—the 10th we found the three Calixto boys, García, Morales and Bermúdez. Things began to look a little better. Bermúdez left us temporarily because he was ill.

The 12th we found Almeida, Chao, Pancho and Che. And the next morning Camilo, Aguilerita and Benítez showed up. The 13th I met Fidel on Marcial Areviches' farm. Faustino and Universo were also there.

The 14th I left with them at eight in the evening for Plurial. On the 13th Fidel had wanted to cross the highway, that was a Saturday. I told him the troops would be leaving on Saturday, I was sure of it, but he wasn't too certain. . . . I led them there and left for a while. When I came back for them they were hiding in a canefield, Fidel on one side, Universo on the other, and Faustino a little further back. Well, on the 14th when we took off and crossed the highway, the troops were gone. On the 15th we reached Monguito Pérez's house.

Then I went back to pick up abandoned weapons. They made a sketch for me showing where the guns had been left. At Ojo del Toro I found rifles that had been left in the care of a comrade who had been taken and executed at Estacadero.

Others had been killed in Ojo del Toro at Capitán's place. A group was massacred by Matico and another by soldiers from Pilón. A soldier who was with Matico organized those executions. It was Manolo Capitán who talked many comrades into surrendering. A shifty character, always looked suspicious to some of us. He was executed when we were in the Sierra. Galleguito handled it. Manolo had told Matico where to find some of our comrades.

—And the death of Juan Manuel Márquez?

GUILLERMO: Juan Manuel was killed at Estacadero. They led him there at night and shot him in a courtyard, I don't know who did it. Some peasants found half of someone's head on a beach—he had been dragged along and knocked to pieces. They also dragged some bodies behind horses over the rocks up to Daniel Pérez' house. Then Regalón had the bodies dumped in a truck. He climbed on top of them and jumped up and down to see if they were really dead. He had his lunch while seated on one of them and cut a finger off another to get a ring. He was eventually executed.

After seeing Fidel I recovered seventeen weapons, thanks to the sketches that had been given me. I was working with Fajardo.

When we were all reunited, we scaled Haitiano peak and came back down toward Caracas mountain. A little before reaching Los Cocos Fidel sent me ahead to arrange for food. I came to a peasant's place, killed a small pig and the farmer gave us some beans. We ate and then slept there until the next day, that is, the 27th. From there we went to a house on Caracas.

On the 28th at eight in the morning, with the lights still on in the house, a plane began circling overhead and the peasant cried, "He's going to fire on us!" He woke everybody up. "A plane! A plane!" Efigenio, Raul and I got out of there. It was the first time I had seen a plane firing. It dropped two bombs which demolished just about everything. It was like something in a movie. Urtimio was the one who guided the pilot.

When we had reached the heights of Espinosa, Urtimio made his appearance. Fidel had assigned him a mission. He had gone to see his family. Someone there was sick and Urtimio had come back with fifty cans of condensed milk. Fidel found that odd because the area was teeming with soldiers. At the time Almeida was captain of the guard. Urtimio had asked him where Fidel slept and all kinds of questions. . . . And on the 28th we were bombed. I still remember. It was terrible.

The next day we moved on to La Hoya. Almeida posted our guards. One of them brought in a peasant and Fidel questioned him. The peasant described the troops and told us where they were going. Fidel asked the guy if he had seen Urtimio and the guy answered he'd seen him on horseback, a prisoner. From then on Fidel really suspected something. With his telescope he studied the troop movements, then said, "They're going to surround us. Break camp!"

We left. Almeida said, "Nobody's to go off on his own. Fidel wants us to arrive there together. Nobody quits the group!" He took charge of the whole group and we arrived at the home of a friend, a Negro, who gave us food. We didn't want to continue on the same route because the army was out there.

We slept on the summit of Puerca Gorda. Afterwards nobody wanted to go on to Lomón. Then Almeida told us, "Whether or not the army's there, we're going. We're going to Lomón because Fidel said we should." We others kept saying it was sure suicide. Well, we went to Lomón and when we reached that "dangerous" place the army was gone.

We reached Lomón seven days after we had left the others. We had shot a guy whose brother was on our side. There were seventeen of us. The twelve of the expedition and five others.

Celia always said, "I'll never forget the execution of the school teacher . . ." Exactly at the moment of execution, after he had taken his place, he saluted Efigenio and said, laughing, "Fire, if you're a man!" Seven of them had been shot that day.

When Matthews arrived, we told him all guard outposts were manned, North, South, East and West. Everything in perfect order. But actually there were only two manned posts. . . . .

Afterwards, Raul arrived. Celia and the others arrived March 19, the beginning of spring. The peasants said there were going to be heavy rains. Fidel told them, "If you see any comrades, tell them we are on the other slope."

I was on first watch when a woman came to tell me some comrades were coming up. Fidel watched them through the telescope and saw they were soldiers. He gave the order to take off once more. The five of us who had not come in the *Granma* went down one side, the rest down the other.

I still remember Hermes Caldero with that cape he always wore. He's one of the most courageous men I have ever known. Hermes was our guide.

And Almeida? In combat he kept shooting all over the place and shouting all the time. People had told him so often that he was going to get himself killed that at El Uvero when he was wounded he shouted, "They've killed me!" But the bullet bounced off the milk can in his pocket. He took out the can and began drinking the milk mixed with blood. . . . .

Chapter Five

FAJARDO

The first one I met was Nico López. He organized the Movement for our area in 1955. I made Frank País' acquaintance in May, 1956 when I went to Celia Sánchez' home in Pilón. Then, on November 30, the signal came to back up the landing. We had practically no weapons. It was at Pilón that I hid in a freezer, as Celia said.

Our immediate superior was Leyva, Almeida's lieutenant. After the collapse of our first efforts against Batista we received orders from Celia to go back to our own places, provided we hadn't compromised our-

selves by becoming too well known. Working in cat-
tle-breeding, I used to be away from my village twenty
or thirty days at a time, so my absence had not at-
tracted attention. But I didn't go back home. While
the others dispersed slowly, three of us, Levya, Rector
and I, stayed in a canefield near Niquero. Then they,
too, returned home and I went to the little farm of an
old pal in the Durán region. That's where I learned of
the landing.

Along with Guillermo García, who worked with me
at cattle-tending, I established contact with fleeing
members of the *Granma* expedition. We both were in
the local peasant militia we had helped organize. That
must have been around December 14.

When Fidel left for Plurial, Guillermo went back
down to find weapons because they only had two rifles
left. We picked up ten abandoned weapons out in the
brush. Among them was a submachine gun of which
I took charge. We also found a Mendoza rifle, a Rem-
ington, a Johnson and a telescopic sight. The army was
everywhere, but we knew every path and could move
all over at will, on foot or on a horse. Until a day when
that was no longer possible.

About December 14 Guillermo met Fidel again. He
led him to Mongo Pérez. Then Raul came with Ciro
Redondo, Armando Rodrígues, Efigenio and René
Rodríguez. They'd held on to their weapons. A curious
detail: Raul with his whole group rejoined Fidel without any guide. When a peasant would tell him, "You
ought to go that way!" he'd go two hundred yards in
the indicated direction, then take off in another one. He

didn't trust anybody. But he did find Fidel his own way.

The first day I greeted Fidel was December 25, Christmas. That was when he told us to gather up our weapons because we were staying in the Sierra. García and I officially entered Fidel's army on December 25.

We dug no trenches, since we were always on the move. When a plane came we'd seek the shelter of a slope and wait for it to pass. Of course, when the second front opened up we changed our tactics because down there we were on the plains.

On December 28 I went into the Sierra with a .22 revolver and twenty-one bullets. Fidel turned the Thompson submachine gun over to me, saying, "That's the pet of the outfit." I kept it until January 1, 1959.

He assigned me to a group and from then on for fifteen months I stuck with those men. I received 149 cartridges. After La Plata only 69 were left, but I got 20 or so more later on. I fired 18 at El Infierno and then only 70 remained again.

We climbed to a place called El Cilantro. I'll never forget one thing: we were scaling a height near Caridad de Mota with Lebrígido as our guide. It was New Year's Day and must have been five in the afternoon. Fidel asked Lebrígido about the mountain up ahead. "It's Caracas," Lebrígido answered. And Fidel said, "Then Batista will not win the war."

I looked around at our "army." We were exhausted, filthy, in sad shape. That was January 1, 1957.

We established contact with Urtimio Guerra, a

peasant sought by the police. It was January 3. Fidel had chosen La Plata as our first objective. We must have been two days' march from La Plata. Urtimio went to Caguara to get coffee and tobacco. That's where Casillas arrested him, at the store.

When they were about to hang Urtimio, Casillas, who was no fool, must have said to himself, "You don't kill characters like this one." He had Urtimio brought down from the scaffold and began talking things over to encourage his betraying us; he offered him a major's commission and 25,000 dollars with a farm and 14 horses thrown in. The farm had belonged to a certain Mendoza whose band had been destroyed, a band for whom Urtimio had been a guide.

After our fight with the parachutists on El Infierno mountain we had to make several long marches to get far enough away. We were poorly fed, hunted like animals. Fidel told Urtimio to look for a place where we could rest twenty days. It was then that Gallego suggested to me that we desert. I went to Che and told him. But Gallego had gotten there first, as soon as he saw I wouldn't go along with his idea. When Che spoke to Fidel about it, Fidel replied that Gallego had already explained that it was to "test the men's morale."

We were preparing lunch when a plane passed over and started wheeling around our area. Fidel said, "Gather everything—in five minutes they'll be shooting."

I was in a hammock, puffing on a cigar of my own making. I didn't move because I was sure that the plane wasn't dangerous. But when it came back, things began jumping like you see in the movies. I leapt from the hammock and went to rejoin the others in a dry creek bed. Now there wasn't one plane; others were coming, five in all, and they fired at the place for four hours. Urtimio had signaled our location to the planes. He wasn't with us because he had gone (so he claimed) to see his sick mother. The truth is that he was in the first plane, showing them where we were.

The first bomb fell on the kitchen but we came out of the whole attack without a single casualty. Afterwards, Casillas came with photographers to "gather up the corpses." He was disappointed because he only found an empty house and some suckling pigs that we were going to roast.

From there we headed for the place of Eligio Mendoza and we scaled El Infierno. At Mendoza's we were rejoined, four or five days after the bombing, by Urtimio. He was wearing a cartridge belt. He said the guards had eaten at his house and forgotten it there. All the houses had been set afire except his. We were happy to have him with us again because we considered him to have better knowledge of the region than anybody else. We were far from suspecting that he was the reason for everything that had happened.

Fidel got to talking with a peasant who told him that he had worked for Celestino, the informer who had been billeting troops. "Why did you leave your place the other day?" Fidel wanted to know. The other man answered, "Because Urtimio told us there was going to be a bombing." That was when Fidel became

suspicious. He asked if there were many soldiers and
the peasant said yes, there were many at Celestino's
and they were expecting reinforcements.

When we reached the height overlooking Celestino's
house we saw that the soldiers were getting ready to
move on. Fidel immediately ordered us to get going.
Ciro Redondo was leaning against a tree when we
heard a branch crack. Ciro said, "Someone's there!"
He got his rifle at the ready and I gripped my submachine gun.

We started off. Suddenly Julio Zénon was loosening
his knapsack and reaching for his rifle. But he hadn't
taken two steps before the first shot rang out. Then
the shooting became a barrage. Zénon fell in front
of me. . . . .

That other time, when Ciro warned us of Matthews'
coming, Fidel told us to whip things into military
shape. I looked at myself and the other guys, our
shoes battered, tied with electric wire, full of holes.
But we changed as best we could and I went up front,
marching like a soldier.

While Fidel was talking with Matthews, Crespo arrived. Raul took him aside, then sent him to Fidel to
announce, "My *Comandante*, we've succeeded in reaching the Second Column." Fidel explained to Matthews
that we were the headquarters unit of the First Column
and the columns were spread across the region. In reality, the whole Rebel Army was right there, in front of
Matthews.

As Fidel spoke to Matthews, Urtimio came into
camp. We knew everything. Ciro was on guard. When
Urtimio came and greeted him, we arrested him. A

comrade now dead, Juventino Alarcón, seized his revolver.

I pointed the barrel of my submachine gun at his
chest and took some papers from his pocket. He
screamed, "Kill me before you read that! Kill me first!"
We took the papers to Fidel and Urtimio rolled on the
ground, saying that his conscience had betrayed him.
He was wearing new army boots. He thought we were
so simple-minded that he could come to us with them
on without arousing suspicion.

He was tried and condemned to death. In the morning, when he was being buried I made a wooden cross.
Che said to me, "You don't believe in it and yet you
are doing that." I answered, "It's so we can find the
place again." I ended up carving a cross on a tree with
my knife.

I never shaved. Crespo and I were the first to start
the fashion. I stopped shaving December 6. And from
May, 1957 on I didn't cut my hair either.

Fidel started wearing a beard a little after we did.
But he never stopped cutting his hair. The first Sierra
Maestra veteran to let his hair grow long was Luís
Crespo. Che shaved his head. As for a beard, he didn't
have one, nor did Raul.

When the Second Front began Raul rejoined us and
said there would be no more retreat. Even if there were
one survivor left we were to hold high the flag of the
Revolution. We had learned what war was like and
we had to press forward because we were to write one
of the most glorious pages of our history. From March
first on Raul commanded the first army to set foot on

the plains. We started out March 1 and reached Guaya-
bal de Yateras on the 28th. There were fifty-three of
us; only forty-two were armed.

Almeida left at the same time for Santiago with
about sixty men. Altogether there were two hundred
men: fifty-three left with Raul, close to sixty with Almeida, and about thirty with Camilo. The others
stayed with Fidel.

In one combat, Carbó attacked a tank by himself
because he had a large-bore gun and thought its shell
could destroy the tank. The tank rushed him and he
ran off. Carrying that cannon of his! It was too heavy
for three men to lift, yet Carbó, all alone, carried it on
his shoulder while running off from the pursuing tank.
He was an extraordinary comrade. A great fighter, far
above most.

It was Luís Montoya who stopped the tanks by killing the lieutenant in the first one. The bullet had
passed through a sight! Since that was the first engine
the others could not move on.

Kidnapping the Americans was the spectacular coup
of our time in the Sierra. In Peña's sector and mine we
captured forty. They were all gathered in my sector at
Yateras. I had thirty-six in a coffee-drying shed. I
looked for thirty-six hammocks and we fed them better
food than we fed our comrades.

I have nothing against them. My personal opinion
of those marines I saw at close hand had nothing to
do with politics. They were the most detestable men
in the world. It isn't my opinion as a *Comandante* of
the Rebel Army but my opinion as a man. Those men

looked down on us Cubans as savages. Even as prisoners, they looked on us with contempt. There was one fat guy who weighed over 250 pounds who kept saying he was in the jungle. "My children must be asking where their papa is, but their papa's in the jungles of Cuba."

There were all kinds of people: Syrians, Puerto Ricans, Mexicans. A real foreign legion of men from everywhere but all out of the same mold. They would undress themselves and come out completely naked on their way to the bathing area. We had to tell the peasant women to stay away from the surrounding field.

I showed them unexploded bombs but they said they weren't American. More than one wanted to get away, and one Mexican asked me how I could stop him from escaping. I retorted it wouldn't be with buckets of water. One day I set up an empty can and fired at it. An American said: "The brave captain shoots well." I added they only had to take one wrong step and they'd see how well I could shoot.

I told them it was dangerous to try escaping because the whole area was mined. Once I dressed a comrade to look wounded and I made them believe it was the result of a mine. That kind of thing held them.

One day at three in the morning I saw the American vice-consul arrive, an ex-colonel from the Second World War. With him was a Cuban who looked just as annoyed. They had received orders to see Raul. The consul only began speaking Spanish later, when he learned he was my prisoner.

When I told him Raul was not there, he announced

through the Cuban, who was acting as interpreter, that he was leaving, since he had been deceived. That was when I told him he could not leave because he was my prisoner. He replied, "This is serious, yes, very serious. You realize what you are saying?" I said I was perfectly aware of it and that, if it was serious, the fact that his government was giving arms to Batista was even worse. He repeated, "It's serious, arresting an American official, very serious." I told him that for me he was only another Batista man.

I went to get a bottle of Bacardi and we began talking more friendly to each other. I asked him to stop saying it was "serious, very serious," because I wouldn't stand for it, I had my orders. But the conversation was more friendly.

The consul wanted to know the political ideology of the officers of the Rebel Army. I answered that my ideology was never to be interested in politics, that I was quite simply a revolutionary fighting for his country's liberty.

We had organized several schools in the region and there was one near us where a young nurse from around Toa taught a class. He asked me what she was teaching the children and I told him it was about Carlos Manuel de Céspedes during our War of Independence. I explained that this interested me very much because I had never gone to school and, for this reason, I wanted to see a time come when no child in my country would go through what I had gone through. He asked permission to see this school, and when he returned he said, "Very good, very good." Later on he sent us 500 notebooks and plenty of pencils.

He also wanted to know what I would do if Russia sent me cargoes of weapons. I told him I'd accept them from Russia as well as from his country if he'd send me any.

An interesting detail: we did not see a single plane on Mount Victoria while the prisoners were there.

Batista's soldiers had their camp on the same range, about forty miles away. I had a telescope and could see all the army movements—even at Guantánamo. I said to the vice-consul that there were troops in the Guantánamo direction and there was a risk of his getting killed. That was why I hadn't sent him to Raul. He answered, "Why didn't you tell me that sooner?" He called the naval base, and twenty-four hours later there wasn't a single soldier in the region. I sent him to Raul with Captain Pereda. Then Comandante Aníbal came and all the Americans left for Caujerí.

That was the most terrible order of the war. It came just when we were worst off. We had repulsed several attacks but had hardly any ammunition left—that was in July. Then we did receive cartridges and, instead of waiting for the enemy offensive, we attacked. And that was the end of happy times in the zone. From morning to night one aerial bombardment followed another. They completely demolished the village of Boquerón. The schools, too. In the countryside nothing was left intact.

In December we had some mobile columns in the zone of operations for surprise attacks against the army. I had 130 well-armed men. They had decided to leave the zone, to organize full battalions and it looked to me like the beginning of an East-West advance. I turned the Yateras command over to a captain and, with the best group, formed the 18th Battalion.

They sent us to take the place of Efigenio's column at the city of Guantánamo. The sole access to Guantánamo was through Camagüey and we wanted to bar entry to the area as well as the exit.

We took the Cecilia road to rejoin Efigenio, Villa and Peña, to prepare for the attack on Guantánamo City January 1. At one place we passed through, people were in the streets, shouting, "He's gone! He's gone!" When I reached Cecilia I learned Batista had fled.

I remained a moment with lowered head, deep in thought, and a lady asked me if the news didn't make me happy. I told her that for us the struggle was going to be much more difficult because until now we had been fighting an open enemy, while in the future the fight would be with hidden foes. Then too, the blood of our dead comrades was not yet dry. Those comrades who had dreamed of this day, of all kinds of projects for the future and yet would never see the victory. . . .

Then Fidel gave the order for resuming the march on all our objectives. We decided to attack Guantánamo City full force that evening. I was going to enter by the San Justo Bridge, Peña by way of Yateras, Efigenio by Santiago, and Villa by Camagüey.

I was going to attack an advanced position of Batista's army. We would open fire at seven in the evening on December 31. Efigenio was going to start off with a .50 machine gun.

The army unit I was going to attack was so placed that I could look down on it from a hill. I spread my men in a ring around the small house where the unit was billeted. They had placed some sandbags at the gate. I posted myself less than twenty yards away.

At the entrance were two soldiers. One was looking toward the city. The other had his feet stretched out on the sandbags.

We were going to open fire at seven. At five minutes to seven a messenger came over from Efigenio to tell us headquarters had notified him that there was to be no more fighting and we were to fraternize with the soldiers. Those two guys had been saved by only five minutes!

We dropped our guns and, on January 2, entered Guantánamo. My column and Peña's were the last to march in. No more resistance occurred except at the barracks.

Casillas commanded the barracks. We put it under siege and Efigenio sent an ultimatum: either they surrendered or we attacked. The whole population was out on the streets. There weren't many soldiers in the area (altogether about two hundred) but they did have enough arms and ammunition to hole up for a year. Finally, Casillas surrendered.

I entered the military post with eight men and we brought out four trucks loaded with guns and munitions which we immediately dispatched to the mountains. We were in the courtyard of the military post when a P-51 plane that we had used on the Second Front flew over, carrying the colors of the 26th of

July. The soldiers were so frightened that they didn't know where to hide. I told them, "Don't be afraid, friends, it's one of ours, and ours don't hurt anybody."

Chapter Six

FAURE CHOMÓN

The early hours of the day we attacked the palace, March 13, 1957, passed without our noticing, that's how busy we were arranging final details. Our greatest fear was that Batista might escape our reach before the start of a day which was to be our rendezvous with history.

At all times a comrade was by the radio, in a corner of the large room crammed with men sleeping on the floor (we had to awaken some of them because we feared their loud snoring would attract outside attention). A comrade carefully jotted down all that he

heard, indicating the exact time. Occasionally he left
his chair to interrupt our conversation and give us information that he judged pertinent. Always the same
comment, "Batista's still at the palace." Once in a
while one of us would leave our group to tell the others
what we had learned.

We spoke about the operation, about the war, politics (the same thing), our plans, the future of the Revolution, Revolutionary Justice (it was to be implacable),
American meddling in Cuban affairs, personal anecdotes; even about art, because we had among us two
artists who had spent their days in the underground
daubing away at canvases they submitted to our criti-
cism. These two painters were Wangüemert and
Briñas.

We recalled the dispute which had exploded a few
days earlier when Briñas had shown us a canvas repre-
senting a woman's head with broken contours. It received our approval, but "Danger" (that was the nick-
name we had given Wangüemert because of his fan-
tastic tricks and his daring) had decided the work
wasn't finished and proceeded to make certain modi-
fications on the still-wet paint with his fingers. The
result had not pleased Briñas, who accused Wangüemert of destroying a magnificent portrait. We had
said that Briñas was right, which only threw oil on
the fire, and the insulted artist had reminded us that
he was a graduate of the academy of San Alejandro.
To which Wangüemert had replied by claiming a very
broad, intensive cultural background in modern art.
After that Carbó and Machadito told another story.

Such was the last scene in that apartment before the attack on the palace, in the command post of the best action group Havana then knew, a group saving the face of the city's revolutionary movement which was weak and badly organized. This was the kind of men who were going to die for liberty by attacking the presidential palace.

Many chapters should be dedicated to the lives of those martyrs who responded to the appeal of José Antonio Echevarría and Menelao Mora. The men in this glorious commando unit were from twenty to forty years old. Some were mature men like Norberto Hernández, veteran of the Spanish Civil War, a great chess player and a fighter ever since Batista's coup. Norberto marched in the first rank despite his strong doubts regarding the attack's success. He found death at the side of men like Ormandi Arenado whose strong outlook I shall never forget. As the 13th dawned, this youthful-looking comrade, a student of architecture, greeted me as if he were about to do the most natural thing in the world. He was so young that I felt like stopping him from taking up arms that day. But my respect for him would not have permitted such a thing.

All were as well-tempered as these two comrades, all those who slept in the two neighboring apartments or went on talking, waiting for the moment to leave for liberty or death.

When day came I decided to go and make a tour of the palace area with Wangüemert. We were very tired, not having slept much the last few days, so we stopped at the Plaza del Vedado and drank some coffee to wake ourselves up a little. A few minutes later we drove along one side of the palace, noting that some cars of the S.I.M. (Military Intelligence Service) were in the nearby streets while another was making the rounds. We stopped before the Beaux-Arts building and Wangüemert went to chat with the police guarding it, to get a little information. He returned and told me everything was normal, the dictator had not left his residence.

For several hours we continued to go around the Palace area, observing the movement of the guards posted outside; we were satisfied to see them so calm. We talked about the stupidity of the agents in the Military Intelligence cars who guarded Batista without taking notice of our bright red vehicle, even though it was circling past them at an hour when traffic was light.

But we soon lost our confidence when we noticed that the streets leading to the palace had been closed off with wooden barriers. We immediately returned to our secret command post and discussed the news with Carlos and Menelao. This measure taken by the palace garrison gave us a jolt because it would be very difficult to attack the palace if we couldn't drive our cars up to the front gate. Moreover, it meant that our plane might have been discovered and the dictator was alerted. We could only expect the worst now.

We returned to the palace with Menelao for a new inspection. We found the barriers still up. But on our return to the command post all was explained by a comrade who had just awakened. He listened to our conversation, then told us that there was nothing unusual about the barriers; he worked for a bus line and he knew that when Batista slept in the palace the barriers were put up to prevent noise which might trouble his sleep. They would be removed in the morning. And that is just what happened around eleven a.m., as predicted by Armando Pérez Pintos.

Without losing a minute, the order was given to get ready to start for the palace. Each man picked up his weapon and ammunition. The assault unit of fifty men was already on a war footing with its arms (25 Thompsons, some M-2s, M-3s and several M-1 carbines, well-oiled, and loaded).

Only two men were deserting us, seized by fear at the last moment. They were kept under guard in Menelao's apartment guarded by Castro Pillalo, who had been wounded earlier, and two other comrades who would help transport him once we went off to the palace. The three were to join us later on. By then a guard on the deserters would no longer be needed.

Soon we brought close to the house the truck that was going to carry most of our comrades. We parked it so that the back doors faced an alley which connected with a service staircase that passed in front of our apartment.

We checked everything. Comrade Loeches, who, along with Jose Echevarria, was going to seize the radio station at the university, would rejoin his team as we departed; twenty minutes later they were to march on to their objective. Each man in our commando team had precise instructions, received with his group in front of a drawing of the palace section to which they were assigned. Each man had his mission, each group its plan.

Close to two o'clock in the afternoon Machadito recited some lines of poetry which filled us with courage and enthusiasm. Forceful words were spoken, words profound in their human and revolutionary content. Carlos Gutiérrez Menoyo said, "We are going to a sacrifice for which there is no reward and which may end in death. I am a grocer. If I come out of it alive, I will only seek to return to my store. Keep in mind that the politicians are on the watch, awaiting the success of actions like ours to profit from them. And maybe they *will* profit. But, no matter what, it has to be done."

We needed a password for communicating once we were inside the palace. I gave one, "Directorate." For the last time we repeated our instructions: everybody had to go into the palace. Nobody was to stay outside because he would become a good target for those who'd be firing on us from the higher terrace and upper stories. Stay close to the wall and advance toward the door. Pay careful attention to comrades ahead of you because a blunder can lose weapons for some of us and cause casualties, too. Once inside the palace, in order to avoid confusion if you have to get out of a room, leave it by the same door you entered.

After that it was time to leave and get into the vehicles. First we brought out the weapons, wrapped in blankets, to keep neighbors from spotting them as we left the building. Then the men started going down the stairs, two by two, and got in the truck. To avoid any accidental discovery we had placed Comrade Tony Castell near the truck to keep a sharp eye out in every direction, while our driver, Amador Silverino, made believe he was polishing the hood with a cloth. When he had made certain nobody was coming, he signaled to a comrade inside and the word was passed upstairs. That was how we brought down two parcels of weapons, one for each car. Then came the comrades assigned to drive. They took their places behind the steering wheels.

The apartments were in disorder, full of hats and jackets we had been told to discard so as to have freedom of movement; and also because we had decided to wear shirtsleeve outfits as the best way of identifying each other in a place where residents and visitors ordinarily dressed formally. Only one comrade preferred to keep his jacket on: Evelio Prieto Guillaume.

Finally it was our turn to go downstairs to our cars. There was Carlos Gutiérrez, Pepe Castellano, Luís Goicoechea, Ubaldo Díaz Fuentes, Wangüemert and myself. We had already been notified by Ignacio González that he was ready. We had a comrade posted across from our building who, as soon as we had departed, was to alert the support team to begin the seizure operation at the radio station.

At three that afternoon Carlos Gutiérrez' auto started the procession, followed by the truck, with our car bringing up the rear. We went down our street to El Vedado district, where traffic was more intense. We continued on a while, then turned toward the palace area.

I remember sitting in the back of the car and watching people walking in the streets, people completely ignorant of what in a few minutes was to set the country on its ears. For instance, that little old lady with the child, perhaps a grandson; or the fat man waiting for a bus, valise in hand; or the baker's helper with a tray of cakes on his head; or that bunch of young girls chatting on a porch; in short, all those who did not know that the passing truck marked *Fast Delivery* and the two cars sandwiching it in were on the way to rescue liberty and happiness from the hands of the assassins. I asked myself how many of those people would grab a rifle and join us, how many would fall in the streets, innocent victims who understood nothing of what was going on.

In our two cars we were bound to fool everybody, even Batista partisans, because there were four in each and we were carrying our weapons practically out in the open, a sure sign that we were part of the forces of repression! With our grenades in our belts we spoke to each other and, even if we smiled once in a while, we all had the same determined expression on our faces. Because of nervous tension, we had just the right military bearing.

Inside the truck the men were crowded together. It was dark in there and the heat was stifling. Everybody was very excited and jokes came from all sides. Evelio had to take off that jacket because of the heat, claiming it was to make sure it didn't get shot through with holes. In the truck's doors there were slits through which Carbó and Machadito could survey the outside. Machadito spotted his fiancée, who glanced at the truck, and he happily announced it to his comrades!

I can truthfully say that during those minutes we felt that this was the most beautiful day of our lives. I believe we all felt it because morale was very high and there was real joy among the men of the commando team. We knew this attack on the palace was a historic event which might liberate our people. And also, it was the great moment we had dreamed of when we were being hunted like animals by Batista's murderers who killed or abducted our comrades after Moncada, up in the Sierra now. . . .

Carlos' automobile was at the vanguard, ours at the rear. We had decided that, if anything happened to the car, Carlos should stop and take care of it while the truck went on, followed by the rear vehicle. If, on the other hand, something happened in back, we should take care of it while Carlos, followed by the truck, continued on. If an obstacle prevented us from reaching the palace, then we were to put the emergency plan into effect. This plan was to head for Police Headquarters, seize it, then capture smaller police posts once we had distributed enough captured weapons. We had decided to accept combat in any case and not retreat from it. If our advance on Police Headquarters was discovered too soon, we would attack the Bureau of Investigations, nearest of all to our starting point. For such eventualities we would have enough time, thanks to our constant listening to the police radio.

Near the palace the shock absorbers of the truck gave out and the rear end was almost touching the ground; one tire was so deflated it looked like a flat. Turning to take the corner of the narrow street of Campanario, the truck scraped along the sidewalk and, on top of that, it had to be maneuvered around parked autos.

There were two different moments when we thought our first contact with the armed forces had begun. The earlier one was on San Miguel Street when a police car came between us and the truck. But it turned off a few hundred feet further on. We had watched every movement of that car's occupants, ready to attack them instantly. The second scare was when the driver of the truck got mixed up and took the wrong street while we lost Carlos from view. We had to retrace our route to find the right street, and chance brought us past the house of the Batista gangster, Rolando Masferrer. Policemen, guards and hangers-on were grouped by the entrance, but we passed under their nose without their suspecting a thing.

Sometimes the truck moved a little away from us because of heavy traffic and we had to increase speed to catch up. Finally we moved into Monserrate Street together, one behind the other. Then we entered Zayas Square, anxiously regarding the palace up ahead of us.

Once again we were cut off from the others. I could see Carlos in Colón Street. I told Abelardo to catch up so we could arrive at the same time. Abelardo, who was a fine driver, was able to maneuver between cars and zigzag around blocking vehicles. We got to

Colón Street behind the truck.

Carlos' car stopped before the entrance to the palace. Ours stopped on his left, between him and the
truck. I jumped out, followed by Wangüemert, Abelardo, Oswaldito, and approached the entrance. Carlos
Gutiérrez, with stunning speed, had already planted
himself in the middle of the arcade. The guards were
so surprised they didn't have time to see the submachine gun spitting at them. In the center of the
portal area, Carlos looked like a cyclops whose thun-
derous blows sent the soldiers tumbling.

Wangüemert and I, advancing to the gate, had to
spray the soldiers who were firing at Carlos' back and
we knocked them out of commission. Castellanos,
Almeida and Goicoechea joined Carlos and fired away.
I reached the porch, too, Wangüemert at my side.
Carlos entered through an open grill gate; this was the
breach through which we entered the palace. Ricardo
Olmedo, who had been riding beside the truck's driver,
jumped out and came over. I leaped to the grill and
grabbed it with one hand to follow Carlos. Suddenly
I felt a light shock. I had the dreamlike impression of
being carried through the air by a giant hand. "Have
I been killed?" I asked myself.

In a few seconds I regained consciousness. I was
stretched out, stunned, on the sidewalk. For an instant I didn't know what to do. Bullets were spattering
about me in such thick bursts I don't know how they
failed to touch me. I rolled against the palace wall.
I can see very clearly what happened. I remember
my arm was numb from a bullet wound. Another

wound, in the hip, was burning me. My liver felt as
if stones had smashed it. At that moment I regretted
not being dead, thinking my liver had burst. Then I
realized the four grenades attached to my belt had
disappeared. I have concluded that those grenades
saved my life by deflecting bullets. The projectiles
must have bounced off, knocking them loose from the
belt. My cartridge clips for the M-3 had disappeared
as well as the revolver I had carried on the hip. The
M-3 also had been knocked beyond reach. The only
thing left me was a pack of .45 cartridges in the rear
pocket of my pants.

My angle of vision revealed a wide sweep of the
action. I recognized some of the terrain and saw a
group of comrades in the middle of the street, firing
up into the palace. They were committing the very
error they had been told a hundred times not to make.
I tried to cry out to them but the uproar was deafening and you couldn't hear a word even from two
yards away.

The palace gate stood between me and my comrades. Bullets were raining on the pavement close to
me. I decided to get close to the others and when the
fire slackened for a moment I crawled toward the back
of Carlos' auto parked by the gate. I got as far as a
bus close to the truck before I was spotted and fired
upon from high up in the palace. I took cover behind
a bus wheel. Particles of metal, plaster and asphalt
burst in my face.

Now I could no longer see where the comrades
were. I thought they must have entered, unless they

had beaten a retreat. I told myself I had committed the same error, getting too far away from the palace walls. I offered an easy target. The shots fired by the soldiers inside kept getting closer. I figured it would soon concentrate on me and I resigned myself to dying because I could not move. I had the impression we were winning, that the victory was going to be ours, and I cursed the fate that had left me disarmed and pinned down by bullets. I would not take part in the triumphal battle within the palace.

I saw Ricardo Olmedo stretched out at the entrance, wounded, and his arm twitching about. Bullets were raining there, too, and it pained me to see he hadn't the strength to move. I could see José Alfonso inside, firing his submachine gun. I was struck by his self-assurance. He fought as if he couldn't possibly be wounded.

The unexpected attack and its force had compelled the palace garrison to fall back. A violent battle did take place on the ground floor, but the guards had turned tail and fled into the upper stories. A .30-caliber machine gun had been abandoned in the courtyard. Now, without stopping their fire, comrades assigned to that task took over the lower level. At the same time others reached the second floor. Once there, they advanced, divided in two groups. Carlos Gutiérrez, Pepe Wangüemert, Luís Almeida, Pepe Castellanos and Luís Goicoechea were seizing the left wing, crossing galleries and halls to the Hall of Mirrors. There they surprised three servants who, astonishment on their faces, raised their hands. Carlos interrogated them but it was time lost because they were practically unable to speak.

Carlos arrived with his group on the North Terrace and saw police approaching. To give them the impression the palace had been taken, he opened fire on them. Keeping up their fire, these comrades reached Batista's office. They had to empty several clips to blast the lock open. Finally they managed to get in, but found no one. The other group proceeded into the right wing in an action paralleling that of the first, engaged in combat with the garrison troops firing at them from the third floor. Menelao didn't stop firing, he moved about with as much agility as if he were the youngest of them all. Delgado and Esperón, entrenched in the gallery facing the court, fired continually with their M-1s at soldiers shooting from upstairs. Machadito threw several grenades, then took his sticks of dynamite—brought along in case we had to blast open a door—lighted the fuses and tossed them one after the other. When these bombs exploded the whole palace shook. They made such a deafening noise that Batista's men, disconcerted, stopped firing. Later we found out they had thought we were attacking with mortars.

One of those dynamite bombs hit a column and ricocheted to fall at Machadito's feet. Luckily it didn't explode. A similar thing happened to Carbó; he threw a grenade at a room, not realizing that a glass door intervened, but the grenade didn't go off. Abelardo and Oswaldito went through one room after the other, searching out the enemy, who was fleeing in terror.

Esperón and Delgado fell dead, next to each other. Machadito was wounded in the thigh. Bullets were ricocheting off the walls and sending glass flying. Menelao was on the ground, unconscious, seriously wounded.

Carlos' group in the left wing established contact with the other one. They identified each other with cries of "Directorate! Long live the Directorate!" On the higher terrace some soldiers responded by cheering the tyrant, which made one think Batista himself might have then come out on the terrace because, before that, the soldiers were silent. Carbó had a bullet in his foot; he had been shot as he got out of the truck with Tony Castell, León Llera and Machadito. He had sustained several bursts of fire which struck the Thompson from his hands and knocked off his eyeglasses. Some bullets passed so close to his face they seared his skin. As he had lost his glasses, Carbó no longer knew what to do—he could see almost nothing. But he did hear Carlos cry, "Forward, comrades, victory is ours!" and had rushed inside the palace where he picked up another submachine gun. He could get around, but soon he was one more wounded man.

Wangüemert ran from one spot to another shooting his M-2. His face and shirt were covered with blood, perhaps because of the glass splinters flying from the windows. Wangüemert was a great fighter, an authentic revolutionary who knew how to add thought to action. So, when the telephone rang, he stopped shooting and picked up the receiver. At the other end of the wire somebody was asking if it were true that the president had been killed. He immediately responded, "Yes! This is a member of the Armed Militia of the University Students' Directorate. We have taken the palace and executed Batista!" A lie at that time had as much value as the truth, because the call could have come from Camp Columbia, from a general or a minister of Batista, and the response might paralyze all aid to the dictator or provoke the flight of his henchmen and so precipitate the regime's collapse.

Briñas fell, a bullet in his chest, and was helped along by Carlos, who was at Menelao's side. Menelao tried to help, too, but Briñas died immediately. Carlos went up a staircase to the third level. He returned, saying, "Boys, the third floor's ours! Advance!" Machadito, who had examined the situation, said to Carlos that they needed reinforcements. Carlos agreed and, with Pepe Castellanos, went through the gallery to reach the stairway and go below to ask the comrades for more men. But he did it so fearlessly that he exposed himself to the soldiers' fire. Carbó tried to stop him, because Briñas had just fallen at that same spot. But it was too late. Carlos and Castellanos were riddled with bullets. Carbó held Carlos in his arms; the last words he spoke were filled with angry determination.

Despite all the time that had elapsed the support operation had not started. Wounded, almost without ammunition, the comrades conferred and concluded that the operation had failed. It was necessary to beat a retreat. For that they had to pass through the area where Briñas, Carlos and Castellanos had fallen.

Machadito shouted, "I'll cover the retreat! When I start shooting run through it fast! I'll follow." And with matchless courage he faced the third-story snipers, turning a continuous fire upon them while his comrades got to the stairway. Batista's guards undoubtedly did not wish to expose themselves to Machadito's submachine gun fire. While our men went down the stairs, projectiles from a large-caliber weapon sent plaster flying barely above their heads. As the comrades pulled out, Machadito couldn't find Carbó and went back into the palace to look for him. Machadito acted like a true hero during the attack. He retreated with Evelio Prieto and another man down Monserrate Street, swinging his fire back and forth.

We had figured that retreat would be impossible if the support operation did not come off, that those attempting to quit the palace would have trouble getting away from the walls of the building. But, although several comrades did fall there, others succeeded in getting out alive. Each one of these individual retreats was a whole operation in itself in which daring, decisiveness and a large amount of luck were all important.

Victory for the attack on the presidential palace would have saved our people two more years of bloody oppression. If it failed, it was not because our plan was defective, nor because there was a shortage of men or weapons before a superior enemy. It was the human factor which betrayed us. We were betrayed by irresponsible men who could not resist flattery, admiration, and the prospects of glory. They took on all responsibilities asked of them, knowing that when it came time to make good their promises they would be incapable of it because they were cowards and boasters. We believed the support operation would take place because those making the promises were considered perfectly competent, some of them being even veterans of the Spanish Civil War. We thought that such men would prefer death sooner than break their word.

I had once proposed Pepe Wangüemert for chief of the support operation. I knew he had the qualifications: courage, ability, a spirit of decision and sacrifice. And his confidence in the triumph of our plan was absolute. Then, too, I had noticed a sort of skepticism in the man to whom we had confided the execution of this part of the plan, as well as a lack of coordination between his lieutenants. I told myself these veterans of Spain were now removed from the years of struggle and found themselves, as one could logically anticipate, at a time in life when they no longer had the same ardor as twenty years earlier. What happened later confirmed my misgivings; many of those veterans participated in actions of this type and all failed.

Carlos and Menelao had been in agreement with me, but had also confessed their fears that, if we named Wangüemert chief of their operation, it would anger those to whom the responsibility had originally been entrusted and, freed of their obligation, they might begin talking too much. It could endanger everything; in brief, it could abort the whole operation. They had thought it was preferable to continue counting on these elements and take the chance of their failing us at the crucial moment, rather than give them an excuse for wrecking the enterprise before it began.

So that was that. At three o'clock when the attack began, Ignacio González, posted on Prado Boulevard with a group of comrades awaiting his orders, had failed to act and, under terrible indecision, walked from one spot to another not knowing what to do. And he had men at hand and was only a few steps away from a truckload of arms ready to support the operation. During that time his lieutenants, Valladares, Morales and others, posted on Lujano Street with a good-sized contingent, delayed giving the take-off signal, even though they had heard on the radio that our operation was under way. The same thing was repeated to them by comrades trying to start them marching on the palace, as promised. They gave various absurd reasons for this delay; for instance, that they could not do anything without receiving a message from Ignacio. . . .

The truck carrying a .50-caliber machine gun did not arrive. Those responsible for it later claimed that it was poorly mounted, that they had gotten stuck in a traffic jam, that the truck had been blocked, that they arrived when the army tanks were already in action. . . .

Despite the failure, this historic gesture shook the dictatorship. Those hours of combat within the palace, as announced over the radio, television, by the press, throughout the island, had made it possible for the Cuban people to envision the possibility that Batista was dead and that his henchmen had taken refuge in the embassies, fearful of popular justice, as it happened two years later.

GOICOECHEA

Chapter Seven

We were supposed to attack the palace on March 11. We expected Batista to celebrate the anniversary of his *coup d'etat* at Camp Columbia, the 10th, and then return to the palace in the early hours of Monday, March 11. Our informers at the executive mansion were to notify us quickly, before three in the afternoon. After three, it would be useless to try anything. We waited for the 11th and nothing happened. Later we learned that our information sources, despite Batista's presence in the palace, had hesitated. The 12th was the same. But the signal did come through on

Wednesday the 13th, before lunch. We were too excited to eat.

So on to the palace. Details of the three-vehicle journey are well known. In a blue Buick, leading the way, Luís Almeida was driving, with Carlos Gutiérrez Menoyo, chief of operations, on his right. I was behind the driver. At my side was Pepe Castellanos. Between three-fifteen and three-twenty we got on Colón Street, which extends before the palace. Our information was that a jeep with a .30-caliber machine gun was parked in front of the palace itself. (In reality, the machine gun turned out to be inside the building, in an inner courtyard, where it was to cause us some trouble.) When we approached the entrance we saw that famous jeep.

We opened all four doors of the car to be able to leap out quickly. It was just like in the movies. As Almeida put on the brakes we jumped into the street. I tried firing at the jeep, but my submachine gun was jammed. At that very moment a bus which had been behind us almost knocked me over. The driver gave a sharp turn to his wheel and avoided me. I pulled out my ammunition clip and put in a new one. During this time, Menoyo had already been spraying the entrance of the guard area with bullets, as Pepe had been doing. We shot down the policeman on duty at the crossroads of Colón and Zulueta Streets.

We infiltrated the guard area. From the seventeen men there, some fled into the courtyard but most, about a dozen, were not able to survive our barrage. They were dead or badly wounded. We suddenly realized that a machine gun was firing on us from the courtyard. One of our men tossed a grenade, but they threw it back out (at least I think it was the same grenade) and it exploded near us.

A shot grazed me. They were shooting from all over, from upper stories of the palace, from the terrace and, with a machine gun, from the Chapel of the Holy Angel. Several comrades blindly rushed toward Zayas Square, and this mistake cost them their lives. Most of them, as soon as they were out of the vehicles, had reached the palace sidewalk, and were entering through the guard area. Or they clung to the walls of the palace, giving us covering fire. We concentrated our own fire on the machine gun until it was silenced. Menelao and seven or eight others were now beside us. Then we climbed the marble staircase on our left to reach Batista's office on the second floor.

At the top of the stairs we turned east and went down a narrow corridor linking several offices, all of them closed. A blonde woman stuck her head through a half-open doorway and cried, "Don't shoot!" then disappeared. Something unexpected brought us to a halt at the end of this corridor: we had obtained a map of the palace but the door now blocking our way was not on it. One of us fired into the door and the lock jumped free. A kick opened the door.

It was the kitchen, and behind it was a dining-room. Three servants in uniform trembled in a corner. On the table were two cups of recently served coffee. I was over-excited and my first impulse was to liqui-

date the three men. I took aim, but Gutiérrez stopped
me, shouting, "Don't shoot!"

The servants told us Batista had just eaten. But
they did not know where he had gone. We searched
them and told them to get into a corner. I jumped over
a table, hopped to the other side and from there inspected Colón Street. The noise of fusillades was terrible. I got back over the table and with my three
comrades went on to the Hall of Mirrors. The others
had gone off in another direction.

The four of us were Gutiérrez, Castellanos, Wangüemert and myself. We had lost sight of Almeida.
Only three of us from the first car were now together
—plus Wangüemert, who was brave as a lion. At the
end of the Hall of Mirrors we reached the door of the
waiting room to Batista's office. Excited voices came
from inside. Gutiérrez shouted, "Come out with your
hands up!" A revolver shot shattering the door glass
was the only response. Carlos pulled a grenade and
tossed it through the broken door. It didn't explode.
We tried another one with the same result. They were
defective—as was the third one we tried. After the
fourth, though, came an explosion.

We broke in, guns blazing. There were two corpses
on the floor. The office was otherwise empty. We
then tried to discover the secret passage which, accord-
ing to a tip, connected Batista's office to his third-
floor apartment. . . . Impossible to find it. How many
hours had slipped by since we had opened fire? How
many minutes? We had lost all sense of time. We
were too busy fighting.

We left the office and ran for a staircase, trying to

get upstairs. Useless: we were under murderous fire from both rifles and machine guns posted up there and on the terrace above. One of our people tossed up a grenade but it came back like a boomerang and exploded a few yards from us. Fortunately we were shielded by the balustrade.

We were running low on ammunition and had to beat a retreat. Returning to the Hall of Mirrors we opened the doors giving out on the north terrace. From there we glimpsed several patrols in autos and other policemen on foot who were firing at the palace from the Avenue of Las Misiones. We opened fire but discovered it was useless because the trees protected them. Moreover, the distance to the targets was considerable. Carlos' submachine gun was jammed and Castellanos' clips were exhausted.

The group which should have been backing us up did not appear. We had to retreat, at whatever cost. We returned to the dining-room with its three servants, who were more dead than alive. One office said on the door: *Telegraph*. Luís Almeida searched it. A telephone began ringing and Wangüemert picked up the receiver. He listened for a second, then replied firmly: "Yes, it's true, the palace has been taken. Batista is dead. We are free!" And he hung up.

Then I saw Machadito with Carbó and a peasant from Pinar del Río who, I believe, had survived the expedition into the second story of the palace. We tried to go down an outside stairway. It was being swept by machine gun fire from upstairs. Castellanos dashed out first. We heard an outburst and saw him pull back to return the fire. But he fell instantly, riddled with bullets. Carlos Gutiérrez, infuriated by Pepe's death, leaped out on the landing, firing away at the upper level. He, too, fell dead at once. We were able to pinpoint the place they were firing from and concentrated our guns on it, reducing the sniper briefly to silence, at least giving us sufficient time to get across the "Death Landing" one by one.[1] I was the last to reach the entrance to the guards' area, which was filled with bodies and blood.

I saw the street, strewn with shells of all calibers, and farther away, Zayas Square and some men on the ground. Wangüemert decided to be the first. He rushed forward like an antelope, followed by Juan Pedro and Machadito. I saw the bullets following their path.

When I began running toward the square I heard some one shouting, "Luís!" Without stopping I turned my head and saw Luís Almeida at the entrance to the palace. I had lost sight of the peasant from Pinar del Río. Nothing was left in me except the instinct of self-preservation. I ran like hell, hearing bullets whistling on every side. I reached the fountain in the center of the square and flakes of cement knocked off by the projectiles fell on me. I plunged my head into the grass, clinging to the basin parapet which was at most a foot high. Sweat made my shirt stick to my skin.

---

[1] The accounts of Fauré and Goicoechea are perceptibly different. But historical exactitude on small points is not what matters most here.

Everywhere there was the smell of powder, blood and death. That terrible odor was to follow me for the next two weeks. I discovered I was pressing the submachine gun tightly against my body with my finger on the trigger.

All of a sudden the shooting stopped. A sinister calm had descended on the square. Without hesitating an instant I rushed diagonally toward Villegas Street. When I reached the corner of Tejadillo Street I heard a man crying out to me, "This way! Go this way!" I turned my gun on him, screaming, "Get lost or I'll flatten you!" That man may have saved my life, because my intention had been to turn at Tejadillo, and there I would have run into reinforcements coming up from police headquarters.

I took Villegas Street. It was then that I realized I had to get rid of my weapon and bullets. At number 13, near a bicycle stand, I saw an open door. I went in. A man and a woman, trembling with fright, had taken refuge there. When the woman saw me she cried, "Don't kill me!" I answered, "Don't be afraid, madam," and I threw aside weapon and ammunition belt. I went out again. I heard an explosion and a bullet dug into a wall at the level of my head. I hurried my steps and, a hundred yards or so further on, I saw a young woman on the doorstep of a building. I went up to her and breathlessly said, "Please, I need to change my clothes." She quickly answered, "I'm sorry but there's only my mother and me in this house. We don't have any men's clothes." Nevertheless, she did ask me in and gave me a glass of water.

I drank and washed my face a little.

I went out again. A policeman was coming out of a cafe fifty yards away. He stared sideways at me but turned at the corner. I controlled my pace. Then I realized that I had automatically taken the direction of the textile business where I kept books and was setting up an accounting system. Six blocks more and I arrived at the store. Outside there were several men and women who stared at me with a strange look. A son of Cossío, one of the owners, gave me some clothes and then drove me to a friend in the Vedado section.

Some days later I was shifted to another house. A month later I was on the farm of an uncle at the town of Jovellanos. Then I went on to another farm, and near the end of the year I joined the rebel troops of the Second Front of Escambray where I stayed until the end of the war.

There was one thing that impressed me very much: while we were on the second floor of the palace trying to get back down, there was an explosion in the middle of a barrage. Then I caught the moving voices of Machadito and Juan Pedro, singing the national anthem. Even now, whenever I think about it, I get a lump in my throat.

Chapter Eight

EFIGENIO

Under fire by mortars and submachine guns, we were able to escape thanks to Comrade Luís Crespo, who had spotted the soldiers encircling us. We had only started off about noon that day in March, 1957, because of Che's attack of asthma which practically kept him from walking. We had been forced to delay our departure from a place called La Emajagua even though it didn't look like a very secure place. Each time Fidel gave the order to move out we had to stop because of Che. We were still there when Comrade Crespo spotted the tyrant's troops moving in. But the crackle of submachine guns and mortars was like a revitalizing tonic for Che and he got going very quickly.

Later he confessed that the best cure for his illness had been the presence of enemy soldiers. But, in spite of his efforts, Che's "gasoline" only lasted him a few miles, and before evening we had to leave him to his fate, waiting for medicine in a zone infested by "khakis," with a kid who couldn't even tie his own shoelaces. After the farewell embraces and handshakes, we left our comrade with heavy hearts to the mercy of possible betrayal or carelessness.

Floundering through muddy fields and paths, pushing on beneath the low-hanging branches of the forest through brush, crossing grass pastures, climbing up and down mountains, we marched without a guide and had to depend on our own vague topographical knowledge. Fidel was leading us toward Mount Caracas, our objective. Caracas is a great, long mountain well over 3,000 feet high, famous for its lush vegetation, filled with wild bees and teeming with flocks of trilling nightingales.

Soaked by rain, damp with sweat and muddy up to the knees, we climbed a steep, green gorge. When we reached the top we saw the incandescent globe which was now to replace Fidel as our guide. Fidel ordered a halt to give us a five-minute rest and began wiping off his glasses with a turned-out pocket. At the end of five minutes he indicated a new direction and we resumed our march. The rain had stopped, but the roads were muddier and muddier. We advanced with difficulty and our boots kept sinking in over the ankles. If the climbs were hard, the descents were no less so. With the one big difference that, if the foot slipped in climbing, the resulting slide set us back a few yards; descending was the opposite and we gained a few yards. That's why mountain people say, "When you are descending, all the saints help you." After seven miles we reached the summit of a mountain, a plateau. A cabin was there, we approached it with great caution.

"Hello, farmer friends!"

"Hello, friends!" answered a man, tall, strong, slender. He had a serene, intelligent look. We were led inside and offered coffee, which his wife was just preparing. As he spoke to us, the fellow practically x-rayed us with those intense eyes. Then he announced, "At first, I thought you were military guards but I certainly see you aren't. Be on the lookout, there was a whole troop here yesterday. For days they have been watching the road." Fidel asked him for more information and whether he could give us anything to eat, fixing his own price. He said he could make us chicken with rice but there was no need to pay. We drank the fresh coffee and, after posting a sentry on a rise to watch the road, we hid in a stream bed several yards from the house.

Time passed and we were sunbathing. After a while the wind brought us the good smell of chicken and rice, almost cooked. Just then Crespo shouted, "Fidel: The guards!" We raised our eyes and across from us, about 500 yards away, saw a file of men apparently armed with rifles, who looked like soldiers. Without waiting to make sure we formed two groups under orders to rendezvous on Mount Caracas. As we left, I heard Camilo groan, "Those bastards won't even let us eat!"

After we had marched close to three miles it began raining and we took a break. Our group consisted of Fidel, Raul, Almeida, Camilo, Ciro Redondo, Julio Díaz, Luís Crespo, Universo Sánchez, myself and three other comrades (all from the *Granma* expedition). The intermittent rains soaked us to the bone and, teeth chattering, we could not stop thinking of that lovely chicken in rice lost to us thanks to those filthy guards. For several hours we didn't exchange a word. Then as night fell, we took off through the fading light on the road to a hamlet we had spotted less than a mile off.

We found it completely abandoned. Fidel decided we would spend the night there. Almeida established the guard duty schedule, then, covered with dirt, we went into the different houses to escape our fatigue and hunger in sleep. The next day, after pulling in our belts a notch, we began climbing a mountain whose height stacks up well against Turquino Peak's, the highest in the island. Three times we halted before reaching the summit. Our physical reserves were exhausted; only our spirit kept us going. Then we followed the crest of a long ridge which gave the impression of being an endless suspended bridge. The peasants of the Sierra call this summit El Firme and consider it the shortest route for going from one place to another. After two hours of such plodding we made a descent which took another hour.

It was then that we came to a stream gushing between great grey boulders. Its water was icy. We refilled our canteens and Fidel ordered an hour's rest; we certainly needed it. We were stretching out when Luís Crespo moved a little upstream to take care of a natural necessity. When Raul realized what Crespo was going to do, he hollered at him, "Hey you, what are you going to do in this stream? You want to contaminate the water?" Crespo came back down and Camilo and I started kidding him. Crespo, who was in bad humor, really got mad and tried to hit me with a stick. Although I dodged, it grazed my shoulder. I felt like fighting back because Crespo was always threatening me, but Raul stepped in and the matter didn't go any further.

At the end of the rest hour, Fidel pointed to a new direction and we resumed our march, following the course of the stream. Then we climbed through a thick forest of great cedars. We passed an illegal sawmill and saw one cut-down cedar tree . . . which, judging by its size, must have been a thousand years old. As we descended another slope through heavy growth, it began raining hard. Whipped by the rain, we hastened our steps and came to a narrow valley where we could see a small cabin. It was abandoned. Adding to our misery, it contained nothing to ease our hunger pains which were becoming more and more unbearable. We bivouacked for an hour.

When the rain stopped Fidel gave the departure

signal; we had to search for food. After going a long way down muddy paths, we climbed to higher ground. Evening came and the sun's red disk sank in the horizon. Not only were we going to sleep with empty bellies again but it would have to be without shelter. Advancing in the growing darkness, though, we did come across another abandoned shack.

Almeida once more assigned the guard turns and I had the last one, from four to five-thirty—the morning of March 10, 1957. I called Almeida over. "Tell me, old pal, what do you have against me? You always give me the morning guard!"

"That's the way it goes," replied Almeida, "it's your turn and that's all there is to it."

"Okay," I told him, "but the next time you give me the same one I don't do it."

"Good, we'll see—"

We were deep in an argument—maybe from bad temper because of hunger, rain and cold—when Raul broke in, saying, "No arguing, comrades. If anybody doesn't want to mount guard, let him tell me. I'll take his place." Raul's words shut me up. I took off my cartridge belt and stretched out with a thousand lice for company. They kept me scratching all night and gave me more trouble than they would give ten dogs.

Just when I was ending my guard, Fidel got up, stretched, gave a big yawn and scanned the horizon with his rifle to test the telescopic sight. Then he took a few steps and started singing, more like humming. Something about nature, plants and dew drops. It amazed me, hearing him sing. I came closer to hear him, but he saw me and said, "Call the others. We're going to explore for food." A few minutes later we were following a small path. Camilo went ahead with that long nervous stride which he kept up even during the longest marches. When he stopped before some thorny bushes blocking our path I was behind him and nudged the barrel of my rifle into his back to annoy him, saying, "All right, all right. What's going on? If you can't make it, let me go ahead."

That was too much for his hot-headed nature. Fuming like a bull stung with *banderillas*, he advanced full force into those bushes. When we later came to a halt and stretched out for a while, damp with sweat and breathless from fatigue, he had the worst scratches, our file leader, although all of us had some left from those thorny bushes. Each time I saw his face and neck, covered with scarlet welts, I felt rotten.

On this path we reached a cabin. Spiderwebs told us that the place had been deserted for some time. We found a little sugar and salt and a very old copy of *Selecciones* which Fidel stuffed in his pocket. A noise inside caught our attention. There were two chickens there! Fidel ordered us to close all the doors so we could catch them. I threw myself on one of them but it escaped, leaving me with a handful of feathers. Then Fidel gave me a lecture, saying I lacked tactical sense, even for catching a miserable chicken. That bird had made me look ridiculous. I couldn't figure out what to say to get myself out of the embarrassing situation when Camilo came along, that eternal smile on his lips and the fugitive chicken now in his hands.

He told us that while chasing the chicken, he came across a peasant who seemed like a nice guy and had offered him beans and other food. He also found out he was going to a store about seven miles off, to pick up provisions. Fidel told Camilo to leave the chicken with me and go see the peasant, take the beans and the rest, and give him money to buy provisions also for us. And to ask him to go fast, we'd wait for him in the shack where we had spent the night.

Rain surprised us and we ran into the shack, soaked and filthy. Almeida gave one of our three comrades orders to hide near the stream, following established security practices. The assigned comrade went off with a sour face. To avoid being spotted by enemy aircraft, it was forbidden to make fires, but we asked Fidel for permission this one time, pointing out that it was late in the afternoon and getting foggy. Fidel agreed, advising us to use dry wood which makes less smoke. A minute later we were warming up inside the shack while a tiny fire gave out smoke like a volcano. The more our skin and clothing dried the more we felt our stomachs flat against our backs. A comrade suggested sharing the sugar to ease our hunger until the dinner which, with the two captured chickens and the other food that was coming, promised to be a veritable banquet.

Almeida was about to pass out the sugar (hardly a pound altogether) but I said, "No, listen, comrades. If you eat the sugar, we'll only be sweetening our throats and stomachs. However, if we make an herb tea with *cañasanta*, we'll be warming up throat and stomach at the same time."

"It's true," said Raul, "I might get rid of this damned cold I feel all the way down into my guts."

Near the cabin there were some *cañasanta* plants. I pulled a clump and we boiled it in an old can. Then, three at a time (we only had three old empty milk cans), we drank this delicious "tea" which seemed better than the best coffee in the world. That was when the peasant sent by Camilo returned.

The peasant explained he hadn't been able to bring all we had ordered because guards were examining the people leaving the store and if they saw somebody lugging a lot of stuff, they took him to the military post and nobody heard any more of him. He had only been able to buy us six pounds of chocolate, two packs of cigars, brown sugar, ten cans of condensed milk and four pairs of boots. Fidel, who needed new boots, lunged for them but it was a great disappointment because none fitted him; he had the biggest feet in the outfit! After distributing the provisions and shoes, Fidel sweat blood as he resewed, with fine metal wire, the soles and uppers of his old boots, which looked like open-mouthed crocodiles.

Our peasant friend warned us to be on the alert because in the store he had heard two policemen talking over a bottle of beer. They said there were only fifteen rebels, dying of hunger, who would be captured any time now that the troops were divided in units of fifty that could better control all the hamlets and roads in the Sierra as well as search the mountains and the brush.

Critical though our situation was, it looked to us as if the guards' prediction was not likely to come true. Drinking beer down on the plain was one thing; taking *cañasanta* tea up in the mountains was another. We were discussing it when Camilo and Luís Crespo arrived, up to their eyes in dirt. They had brought a chicken, an old duck, some mushrooms, a handful of garlic, some *culantro* leaves, pimentos, and two pounds of kidney beans.

Camilo told Fidel that, on the way, he had found our sentry, Perico, sleeping by the stream. "If I'd been an enemy, I could have captured him without a shot." Fidel was angry and sent someone to get Perico. He chewed him out and gave him a whole night of guard duty. Camilo and I wanted a more severe punishment for him. Later on, though, we laughed over Perico's frightened look as Fidel bawled him out. We realized his morale was down to zero, like some others on whom we could no longer count. Fidel himself knew it.

As I was the one who had the most culinary knowledge, I prepared the meal, with some help. In a can, we made soup with beans and king bananas plus the garlic and some *culantro* leaves. In another large can we began cooking the three chickens and the grandpa duck. With lots of seasoning. Then all of us, by the fire, quietly watched the tongues of flames licking the sides of those cans. We looked like priests about to pay homage to strange gods. The aromatic vapors increased our pangs tenfold. Only the thought that we would soon be eating gave us the courage to endure that torture.

Two hours later it seemed to me that the beans

were cooked. Fidel told me, "Serve the soup, but keep the chickens simmering and save them for tomorrow."

When Camilo heard that he started groaning, "What? Hungry as we are, they're going to keep the chickens for tomorrow? They're crazy!"

Each comrade had two canfuls of soup. It was so good that one of them assured me he had never eaten better even in the best restaurants. The chickens and their brother duck continued to cook. Those who, like me, had disagreed with Fidel's order, now feeling their bellies well-stuffed, agreed he had been right. Afterwards, a good coffee that had been strained through an old but clean sock, plus a cigar, restored our morale. It made me remember, somewhat inexactly, a sentence attributed to Napoleon, "The best way to a soldier's heart is through his stomach."

Some time later our romantics began daydreaming and making plans for the future. Almeida said, "When the war's over, I'm asking leave to go to Mexico to meet my fiancée and marry her."

Then Crespo, a good peasant, said, "As for me, boys, if I come out of this alive, I'm going to have a little account to settle with an army corporal. At a dance in my village he slammed me and a few other men with his saber and socked us around—after he took my girl from me!" He added, "I'll smash him to a pulp, boys. As for her, just jilting her'll be enough."

Camilo said, "When the war's over, I'm taking a little rest, then I'm organizing an expedition to Santo Domingo against Trujillo's tyranny."

We were talking to while away the hours. Some of us wanted to be farmers, others engineers, politicians, soldiers, etcetera. Then one comrade, a more realistic one, pointed out, "After the fight at El Infierno we were almost wiped out three times. Just two days ago it was only a question of hours whether we'd fall into a trap. And here we are now, practically surrounded and with only twelve rifles and forty rounds of ammunition."

At this point Fidel broke in. "Comrades, it's true we almost were destroyed three times; it's true the enemy threatens us everywhere; it's true the enemy tries to deny we're still alive before the Cuban people; it's true we only have twelve rifles and forty rounds for each weapon. But it's also true that Frank País will keep his word; it's probable that right now he's on his way from Santiago with an armed contingent. It's also true that not long ago in place of twelve guns and one victory to our credit, we had only seven guns and no victory at all. We are back on the march, comrades. It's also true that the terrain here prepares the way for our wiping out the tyrant's best troops before going down into the plains and cities to conquer them there. And if, despite everything, if despite all that we still must die in combat, it won't be without having opposed the enemy in a resistance worthy of the ancient Spartans. And remember, comrades, even the children of our enemies will have to take off their hats before the peaks of our Sierra Maestra."

Silence gripped our hearts. We were deeply moved by the words of our leader.

It was still raining. A strong wind was blowing and the cabin door let in violent blasts of damp, cold air. A comrade complained, "Why doesn't this damned cabin have a real door!" But we had no reason to complain. We were lucky to be sleeping with full stomachs, heat from a fire and a roof over our heads. Still, man is never content with what he has. And that is what has made him the colossus he now is, superior to all creation in power, courage and intelligence.

Soon almost all of us were asleep.

Around dawn someone awakened me. He handed over the wristwatch with a luminous face, saying, "You've got the last turn on guard. At five-thirty sound reveille."

"Okay," I answered. I got up and went to the assigned place, sliding and tumbling along the dark path which sloped down to the stream. For mounting guard I chose a large tree trunk, about ten yards from the stream. But even though rain had stopped falling, the moss covering the trunk was soaked with icy water. When my eyes got used to the dark, I picked out a little rise to the right of the path, dumped my knapsack and cloak on the ground, and sat down in my shelter, my back against the embankment.

From time to time I looked at the luminous dial of the watch and found that the hands were advancing very slowly. In the middle of my watch I heard a weird noise to the left of the path. Without making the least sound I released the safety on my rifle and began listening, while a weak beam of moonlight

between two clouds lighted the area enough for me to
spot any dangerous shadow. I saw nothing. The moon
disappeared, total darkness returned and I again heard
the noise, like steps, nearer to me this time at the
place where the path swung away from the stream.
. . . I was getting ready. I knew what I had to do; my
duty was to warn my comrades if I had the time and,
if not, to fire on the enemy, which alone would alert
the others.

The seconds passed and I said to myself, "Is it possible that those dogs are capable of making night com-
mandos, like us? I doubt it, but still—" Some minutes
later the noise once more, still closer, about thirty
yards away. I was now sure that something live was
moving out there. I thought of getting back to the
cabin to alert the others, but what if it were nothing?
What a howler that would be! I continued to wait, my
index finger caressing the trigger of my rifle. Even
if they attacked me with a knife, I'd have time to get
off at least one shot. The singing of crickets and frogs
annoyed me; I was cursing these creatures for their
stupid music when I caught a noise so close by now
that I almost emptied my clip at it.

The noise came anew, accompanied this time by a
light, guttural cry. I held my breath, anxiously waiting, when I remembered something I had seen as a
child in a film. The hero, trying to guess the position
of his enemy in the darkness, threw a stone out to
make noise, and when his enemy fired in the direction
of the sound, he fired at the blazing gun and thus liqui-
dated his adversary. I instantly took a stone from the

path and threw it toward the stream. Then I heard something moving off and I could tell it was an animal. Maybe a wild pig.

I regained normal breathing, threw the safety back on and rested the rifle on my knees. Fine droplets of night-dew fell on my cap and weapons. I wanted terribly to smoke a cigarette, but smoking on guard duty was strictly forbidden. An hour went by. Morpheus had several times brushed my eyelids. But this was not a time for sleep. I got up to walk on the path a little and drive the drowsiness away. Then I came back and sat down. To avoid dozing off, I began counting the seconds. When I reached sixty I started all over. . . .

. . . Then, when I again looked at the luminous dial of my watch, I saw with astonishment that it had swollen to enormous dimensions. Now the diameter was at least five yards. More than that, I was trapped by this enormous dial. Throat tight with fear, I tried to get out of this strange prison. My hands were touching the ceiling of glass and I was marching on the huge metallic green numbers. Now a loud tic-tac resounded in my ears like cannon shots driving me crazy while to add to my misfortune, I saw the two fluorescent hands advancing toward me. The hands seemed like two gigantic pincers closing in on me. It was a terrifying situation, I had to do something to get out of there. I searched for my rifle in vain; the huge hands kept getting closer and closer to me. Of all the ways to die, flattened out like a Mexican *tortilla* seemed the worst to me.

The hands were now two yards away from each other, I had to come to a decision and throw myself with all my strength against one of them, feet solidly digging in the floor, hands gripping it tightly; but I realized now that the hand was dragging me toward the other, like a feather. Finally, I felt both hands clasping my body. Everything was over and . . . when I woke up I was pressing my rifle full force against my chest.

I had not been able to flee that nightmare because I had fallen soundly asleep. I was ashamed of myself, I who a few hours earlier had asked a more severe punishment for a comrade who had also fallen asleep on guard duty! . . . That's why, comrades, before you judge a soldier who sleeps while on guard duty, you should think twice. It can happen to you! I looked at my wristwatch, it was five-thirty, time for reveille. Dawn was breaking and the nightingales announced a new day. I went to the cabin.

Fidel was the first to get up. After yawning and stretching, he said, "And those chickens? Are they tender enough?"

"Yes," I answered, "so tender that the heat has turned them into *paté*."

"Fine," said Fidel, "divide it up and then, right after, we're leaving."

We ate the delicious pulp. Then Fidel gave us a fix on the way to Caracas that turned out to be pretty accurate. . . .

At the end of two days of marching (plus one night of rest) we reached the first outcroppings of the

famous mountain. It was March 13, 1957. We found
our old camp where one month earlier B-26s had
wakened us one morning, unloading a good hundred
bombs on us plus thousands of .50-caliber projectiles.
But although we had been awakened from sleep that
time, we suffered more from fright than actual harm.
I still remember perfectly that Raul, Ciro and I had
chosen for our refuge an enormous white boulder, and
when we got some yards from it a frightening din
broke out and the enormous rock broke up in clouds
of smoke and fire: a B-26 had unloaded its cargo
there. We had escaped by only a matter of seconds!

Now we were bivouacking in the same place, recall-
ing all those moments of anguish and emotion. Camilo
joked while holding a fragment of the bomb that
had exploded in our kitchen. Fidel asked Universo
for the portable radio to listen to the news, as was his
custom. We were very far from thinking that at the
same moment in Havana, in the very palace of Ser-
geant-Criminal Batista, there was taking place one of
the highest feats of heroism and courage in the history
of our country, already rich in great exploits! Fidel,
holding the radio close to his ear because the batteries
were weak, played nervously with the dial, when suddenly his face lighted up as if an electric current were
running through him. He leaped to his feet and said,
excitedly, "Something magnificent is happening in
Havana!"

The news came through, little by little. Then we
were saddened to learn of the deaths of some close
friends. After praising the heroism of the palace ex-

ploit, Fidel told Raul to remain in camp while he went with Camilo and me to the summit of Caracas, to look for a written message that was supposed to be left there for us if the reinforcements promised by Frank had arrived.

With Camilo in front and me in the middle we started off. At one point Fidel saw that Camilo had lost his way and he became angry. "Let me go ahead, you're always fouling things up." He took the lead. Camilo and I told each other that, considering what could happen, it was not safe for Fidel to march ahead like that. But by then we had reached the place Fidel had indicated. It was a large tree at the top of Caracas. Fidel recognized it and, after rummaging in a hollow under the trunk, he saw there was no message.

We asked each other, "Is it still possible for the reinforcements Frank promised to come if they haven't arrived by now? It *isn't* possible. It must be over two weeks since they left Santiago. What's happened to them?" As night was falling and it was too late to get back to camp, Fidel decided to spend the night there. We chose the old wall of a long-abandoned camp for shelter. Rain threatened and the wind blew hard enough to uproot a tree. The cold made us huddle as close as possible to each other. The best protected was Fidel, who was in the middle. We fell into deep sleep without giving a care to guard duty. The next morning we rejoined Raul, then went off in the direction of Juana, a spot not very far away. There we were likely to find the comrades from whom we had separated the day the guards had deprived us of chicken and rice. Maybe the long-waited-for reinforcements from Frank País would also be there. . . .

After half a day lost in detours and climbing, Fidel finally found the right way. Close to midnight we reached the home of some peasant friends and were surprised to find Che, Guillermo, Ramirito and a comrade we didn't know. Che told Fidel his odyssey from the place where he had left him ill. When Fidel asked about the unknown comrade, Che told him he was part of a contingent of eighty armed men sent by Frank from Santiago. "How many did you say?" asked Fidel. "About eighty, with rifles, submachine guns of various calibers and several carbines." "I was sure we could count on Frank," nodded Fidel. "Che, we have to carry off some big blow against the tyranny, something to make them understand they can't go on denying the existence of this large a force in the Sierra Maestra. Especially since Batista said our interview with Matthews was a fraud."

Che thought for a moment, then replied, "I'm in complete agreement, Fidel, but it's absolutely essential that this blow be a victorious one, that we take plenty of weapons and that we inflict on them such heavy losses that it will become impossible for the government to hide the truth."

Chapter Nine

CAMILO

Fidel and Comrades, I embrace you all after an involuntary silence brought on by the thousand mishaps of our nomadic existence. Today, after infiltrating thirty miles into Las Villas Province and finding a well-organized, if poorly equipped, Rebel encampment with good people, I finally have the opportunity to send you the report which you should have had long ago in your possession.

To begin with, I will tell you that from the time we quit the Cauto zone we marched every single night to the west. Forty nights of marching, often without scouts, using the south coast and a compass to guide our movements. Travel along this coast was disastrously bad. For fifteen days we went through water and mud up to the knees, spending nights avoiding ambushes from troops stationed in our path.

During the thirty-one days of travel across Camagüey Province, we only ate eleven times, even though this is the most important cattle-raising section of our nation. After four days of total starvation, we had to kill and eat a mare from our meagre cavalry. Almost all of our animals remained behind in the mud and marshes of the south coast.

As for Che, it is now twenty-two days that we are without news of him. Our last information dates back to the 16th of last month when eight comrades, plus another who came in later on, joined up with us after a battle at the place called Cuatro Compañeros.

Yesterday, we arrived in this Rebel camp where we were wonderfully received. The Comandante, Señor Félix Torres, has given us the utmost attention. Ahead of Che's coming, they have posted guides all the way to the provincial boundary. In the same zone there is also a 26th of July group with which we have made contact.

Today they told me that Che has quit the Baragua region. But he is advancing slowly because his men are in bad physical condition. However, this news has not been confirmed. Having passed through the same region, we know it well. A terrible place; on one side the sea and swamps, on the other the Lituabo River with only one bridge over it, the one at Cantarranas, where there are three enemy roadblocks set up a half mile from each other, each with twenty men. To the north, the Central Sugar Refineries of Baragua, Jagüeyal and Stewart, full of soldiers and numerous traps. On the other side is the Baragua line to the pier area by the same name. It has many roadblocks and ambush setups, erected since we passed through. The government has concentrated more than seven hundred soldiers there. The army's tactics had been to let us advance toward the Lituabo, then cut off our route and deliver a crushing blow. They didn't want the Antonio Maceo column to reach its goal.

During our crossing of Camagüey, we had three fights with Batista mercenaries, but suffered no losses. However, Lieutenant Senén Meriño was captured during an expedition in the rice-growing area of Aguilera, trying to locate a guide for us. We also lost Lieutenant Delfín Moreno, the one who carried messages when we were operating in Cauto, our first descent into the plains. He had been surprised by soldiers in a house with Comrade Germán Barrero (El Abuelo) who was able to escape but did not know how to re-establish contact with the column. We lost a great quantity of documents, among which was the log of our two months in the plains.

This happened because the main body of our troops could not reach the rendezvous point on time. Our guide had lost the way for more than two hours in a sugar-cane plantation. Daybreak caught us within view of many houses so we could not risk moving on. That was the day after we crossed the Júcaro-

Morón lines and smashed the aqueduct at Ciego de Avila after a fire fight in which we killed an army corporal, took a prisoner, and seized two Springfields, two cartridge cases and two revolvers.

And now a detailed report on the most important events during our crossing of Camagüey Province.

We crossed the Jobado in the south on September 7 before midnight. The next day we skirted an emplacement which was constructed against an armed group that their intelligence indicated was in the area. Those were the guards with whom Che had a run-in when he passed through there. We reached a forest without incident. For two hours in the morning we heard sporadic gunfire, which made us think the army was advancing on the way we had followed the preceding night.

Not long afterwards, a messenger from Che informed us that his men had been in combat with the army. There were two dead and one wounded in our ranks, two dead in theirs and five of them our prisoners. Che's column had taken seven rifles. Then it linked up with ours and together we reached the forests around the Francisco sugar mill.

The night of the 10th we left behind our cavalry (altogether sixty mounts) and went ahead in trucks. Less than a mile from the rail line of the Francisco mill our advance patrol under Captain Guerra caught sight of a vehicle filled with soldiers. We immediately took the necessary measures, believing that the army had set up ambushes based on their knowledge of the route we had so far taken. In the afternoon 250 soldiers arrived from Camagüey. We cut the telephone cables and moved into combat positions. The military vehicle then took flight and we crossed the railroad tracks as quickly as possible. A river in flood brought us to a halt and we had to camp in a forest.

The following night we went on in different trucks. After strenuous efforts to get the trucks out of deep mud we reached the Santa Cruz-Camagüey highway, a road well guarded by enemy patrols. After about a mile on this highway we took a track leading to the village of Cuatro Compañeros. We soon learned that an enemy unit was on our trail. We took the necessary measures for a fight but no battle was joined. We were ready, at the first shot, to blow up the road and cut the telephone lines from Camagüey to Santa Cruz. At seven that evening we left the woods. A few miles on we reached a bridge, but we had no sooner passed over it than we heard a strong explosion followed by bursts of submachine gun and automatic fire. We threw ourselves on the ground and Captain Guerra's advance force answered the enemy fire. The house from which the shooting came was encircled and the Batista men withdrew with their wounded, a number we couldn't determine although they left many traces of blood. The courage and decisiveness of our guide should be mentioned here.

The afternoon of the 16th we received a group of nine comrades who had lost contact with Che's column. Three were officers. From that day on they marched with us. These nine comrades brought with them two young men, armed with hunting rifles, who had guided them to us. These two turned out to be the ones who were robbing and pillaging in the name of the 26th of July Movement. Edel Casañas, 17, and Maximino Quevedo, 29, were found guilty of armed assault and robbery and, unable to deny the charges, were condemned to death.

The 18th we reached the place where we had planned to cross the San Pedro after a reconnaissance by our patrol. Enemy troops with two cannon were at the river's mouth in addition to 200 soldiers and several outposts on the Castillo estate. We crossed the Altamira, which was in flood, with the aid of rafts. When we reached the place where we were to rest several days, our position was discovered by two men who fled. They turned out to be soldiers.

The morning of the 20th we reached a little woods on the Trinidad farm two miles from the Yegua River; en route we crossed the Vertientes highway and the rail line from the Agramonte mill to the coast. Soldiers had set up emplacements on the road to the beaches. There were altogether 600 mercenaries.

On the 21st we slipped through the line of emplacements extending from Santa Maria Beach to the Agramonte mill, not far from the tracks where patrols swept through every ten minutes. We were able to pass between two patrols. One comrade fell from his horse, setting his rifle off. Some days later we learned from a prisoner that a group of soldiers had seen us at the place where we crossed and had heard the detonation of that gun but had not made the least effort to stop us. This is striking proof that Batista's army does not want to fight and that its morale is getting lower and lower.

That night we camped at Un Guanal, near to the line which goes to Florida. There were 150 soldiers two miles away from us. At noon we heard some shots and the roar of several railroad cars, bearing troops destined to cut us off farther on. That night we slipped across the railroad tracks between Santa Maria and Florida, without the least trouble from the patrols.

Wednesday the 23rd Lieutenant Senén Mariño, accompanied by a prisoner named Hernández, went exploring for a guide because we were lost. That afternoon some planes heavily bombed a small forest several miles from us. Comrade Senén did not return; he had been captured by the guards. We learned later that he conducted himself like a true revolutionary and did not give our location away to the enemy.

The situation grew progressively worse as we proceeded without a guide. Consulting our compass, we marched two nights along the coast. At the end of the second night we were lost again. We set up camp in a wooded area. Lieutenant Delfín Moreno was posted a mile farther on in the woods with his men. Their orders were to stop the first peasant passing along the road there so he would guide us and furnish us with news. When morning passed without anybody going by, he entered a building in the rice-fields and found three workers.

He explained that he was lost and needed somebody to get him out of there. One of the three men, one called Sanabria, a tall, round-faced Negro, offered to go and get somebody who knew the region. He was, in fact, a police informer of the vilest kind. Instead of going for a guide, he brought the guards down on us, preventing us from finishing the mare, our sole nourishment after four days of starvation. Lieutenant Moreno rejoined us, leaving the tyrant's soldiers to pass the next twenty-three hours laying down a heavy gunfire curtain on the woods in which nobody remained.

Guided by the rice-workers, we got away from that place while Batista's soldiers, with rare courage, kept up their battle in the deserted woodland! We reached a charcoalmaker's hut, where we found five worthless men. One of them even broke out bawling. But, our situation being so difficult, we had to force them to guide us from that area. They led us to a forest, where we bivouacked and listened to the distant din of the "battle."

A patrol located a house where, besides some food, we found a man to guide us two miles onward. A region truly poor in guides! That night we crossed the tracks which run from the Baragua mill to the dock area by the same name. A few miles from there we found another guide of whom we were not too sure but who could lead us to the Lituabo Bridge. This was the sole way of getting over because the river could not be forded and the swamps along the coast were impassable. Knowing we couldn't reach a safe camping area before daybreak once we crossed the bridge, we decided to bivouac on this side and send a scouting party into the unsafe area. We were anticipating dan-

ger because the game-keeper of the area was a good-
for-nothing who had sold out comrades during the
August 5 strike and because patrols had been stopping
all travelers for the past three days and were trying
to pick up our trail.

At three in the afternoon our sentries surprised
three men dressed like peasants. After long, separate
interrogations they started squealing on each other.
In any case, two of them were wearing army boots
while they denied being part of the military forces.
The youngest, named Enrique Navarro Herrera, was
the game-keeper in question. When we told them that
they were going to march ahead of us on the bridge,
they confessed everything. One was Corporal Trujillo
Medina, the other, Private Jesús Barrios. Navarro Herrera, a real stool-pigeon, was serving as guide for the
two spies.

Corporal Trujillo explained in detail about all the
outposts that five companies (more than 500 men)
had set up in the bridge area as well as along the
tracks to the Baragua mill. Even if we got through this
front, we would find others as far on as Stewart, and
between Stewart and Júcaro.

As it was, Corporal Trujillo, who had placed these
outposts, was the man who best knew the zone, having served in it for thirty years. We explained to him
that the only way he could save his life would be to
get us through without conflict. The one way to avoid
an ambush, he told us, was to march north and cross
the Central Highway fifteen miles away, not far from
Ciego de Avila. Without any doubt, Corporal Trujillo

turned out to be the best of our guides. He brought us, without any difficulty at all, through innumerable outpost areas and past the Baragua barracks, where there were over two hundred soldiers. After having marched over twenty miles (due to all the detours we had to make) we reached the Central Highway near morning and camped in a sugarcane field a few hundred yards away.

That morning we sent our medical officer to Ciego de Avila to make contact with the Movement's leadership and to obtain equipment, medicine, guides and trucks, all of which we needed to continue our uncertain journey to Las Villas.

Under a beating rain we waited for midnight. Already they were aware in Ciego de Avila of our presence. Considering the dangers the area presented for us and the lack of shelter, we had decided, despite the late hour and the bad condition of the roads, to requisition some trucks and get as far away as possible. And this despite the attention the trucks would call to us by constantly getting mired in the mud.

Around twelve-thirty they brought us some trucks from mills in a small village and we started off, stalling in mud time and again. So much time was wasted that daybreak caught us close to another bunch of houses; we had to take the place with its thirty houses. The inhabitants were at first terrified (they expected to see the army appear at any moment) but they quickly calmed down and talked with us in a friendly manner. We posted sentries far enough away to avoid exposing the villagers to danger, but in large enough numbers to check the enemy. We were very conscious of the danger that the army's approach on the village could present, of how one of its barbaric outbursts could bring on a massacre of the inhabitants.

In the school there were more than forty children and at first all were crying, pining to go home. That day their school teacher was absent, due to the bad state of the roads. A Rebel, Captain Antonio Sánchez, was put in charge of running the class and distributing refreshments, candy, pencils and notebooks. It ended up with everybody very happy. For our part, those hours near the children were touching. They allowed us to forget a little the pain and fatigue of the preceding days. When it came time for them to return to their homes one of them asked that we take him with us or come back the next day. They all sang the national anthem and promised us to put flowers every Friday on the bust of José Martí in the school and ask their teacher to tell them about him and the ideals for which he died.

That night we were to cross the historic road from Júcaro to Morón. Filled with patriotic fervor, the men looked forward to getting under way. At exactly seven we started pulling the trucks out of the mud. It was twelve-thirty on the morning of September 31 when we crossed the trail. The men went on foot, the trucks behind. As we were running low on gas, we went looking for it near the aqueduct of Ciego de Avila. We wrecked the waterworks, leaving the town without water for the next few days. Our forces immediately took to the trucks, but after being driven a few miles, the trucks broke down in mudholes and we had to abandon them because it was almost daylight. We found a mule driver who volunteered to lead us into a forest where we could spend the day. As it was going to be necessary to take the loaded mounts by another route, Lieutenant Delfín Moreno and Private Germán Barrero were ordered to lead them to an assigned location, while the main body of our troops would take a few shortcuts to the same place, which was to be our next camp site.

After two hours of marching through canefields our guide lost the way and it was impossible to go on. There were many houses nearby. We decided to camp out in the fields and wait for night before resuming movement. At seven in the morning a reconnaissance plane spotted the abandoned trucks, less than two miles from the spot where we now found ourselves. At eleven-thirty our scouting patrol caught sight of a large number of soldiers searching the banks of the river we had crossed only a little while before. At the same time six truckloads of soldiers appeared on a mud road a half-mile away. About noon many guards passed close to our advance unit. All the men, in a state of alert, regrouped in a defensive line that stretched the length and breadth of our canefield. The sun beat down hard but none of the men budged for fear of giving away our position.

At four we heard heavy firing three or four miles away. The comings and goings of the trucks told us that the soldiers were trying to find our position, a position which offered few advantages. The reconnaissance plane passed overhead several times. When night came we had to cross a very dangerous zone; we had no idea where the enemy might be. Precisely at seven we started and, after several hours, were out of danger.

We all wanted very much to find the two comrades separated from us and the same thought occurred to all: were they the people the soldiers had fired on that afternoon? That, as it turned out, was actually what had happened. A truckload of soldiers had reached a house where the pair were stopping, and Lieutenant Moreno was killed. Private Barrero, who was outside the house at the time, succeeded in escaping. This serious carelessness cost the life of one of our bravest and most efficient men. At the same time we lost certain documents and our road log of the months we had operated in the Cauto zone.

Profoundly grieved by the loss of our comrade, we resumed our march and at four in the morning camped in a forest. Taking all possible security measures, we revealed our presence to no one. We did not even forage. Our sole aim was to reach Las Villas Province and, as we were not very far from it now, that gave us renewed strength.

That night we crossed the Marroquí-Majagua road. In this zone we found more committed elements who were ready to cooperate with us in one way or another. In camp we had many visitors, three of whom joined up. That made a total of seven recruits, including those who joined in Camagüey. We received so much aid that several days later, when we crossed into Las Villas, some comrades were still carrying two rifles each. While at that encampment, we learned of five young men traveling by car from Marroquí to Majagua who were killed by the tyrant's troops. The preceding night some military trucks had passed the car and, each group, taking the other for rebels, had opened fire. Result: five dead, several wounded and many runaway soldiers who were only regrouped the next day. These soldiers said they had been attacked by a large Rebel contingent and forced to seek aid and protection from the inhabitants so that they could be guided to the nearest military post!

That night we marched little and ate much. At two in the morning we reached the so-called Mountain of the Americans. The rough terrain reminded us of our beloved Sierra Maestra and our dear comrades who, hundreds of miles from there, were following us in their thoughts. The next morning at seven we took the road to Las Villas. The cowardice of our guides was making it all the longer for us. One of them, a certain Jesús López who had volunteered to accompany us, kept himself armed with a Winchester and a revolver. He had sported these a long time to show his revolutionary spirit but took flight upon learning that en route there were two outposts of forty soldiers each and that we were going to pass between them. The mistake of another guide almost took us to Florencia. That night we encamped barely two miles from Las Villas.

Day rose cloudy and rainy. This had been our only night of rest after forty days of marching. The Jatibonico, in full flood, did not permit us to cross and we had to return to our encampment under torrential rain accompanied by strong winds. We occupied several houses there and passed the night. The next day, as we prepared to eat, news kept breaking around us: the army was approaching, the soldiers were spreading out on all sides, the roads had been cut, the soldiers from Ramones, Boquerones and Florencia, in a great joint maneuver, were getting ready to cut the highway and encircle us.

Nothing was going to stop us now, neither rivers in flood nor hundreds of soldiers. To the Jatibonico! A rope was stretched across. The water came up to our chests and the current was powerful. When I reached the other bank, I kissed the ground. All of our comrades were very excited. We had fulfilled one small part of our mission. We had left behind us the Province of Camagüey, its dangers, its hunger. To have an idea of what it had been like, just remember that during the thirty-one days of crossing the province, we only ate eleven times, including the day we ate the mare, raw and unsalted.

Thus we had accomplished one of the greatest revolutionary exploits on the military level. Despite the forces deployed by the tyranny to exterminate us, we had gone all the way from Oriente Province to Las Villas with the loss of only three men.

Signed: Camilo Cienfuegos

P. S. It is late and the bearer of this message has been

waiting here since morning; today planes dropped leaflets announcing a bombing.

As soon as I have news of Che, I will write to you, now that some contact has been established. You will be regularly informed of our march which has so far taken longer than expected. We made every effort to gain time but it was impossible.

Here in camp there is a son of our friend Cuevas whom we are going to enroll. En route we had to leave five comrades behind in secure places because their physical condition did not permit them to go on.

I am certain we will reach Pinar del Río. We are all very determined to do so. At no time has anybody weakened either physically or morally. Hunger, sleeplessness and the many dangers only helped strengthen our determination.

This is a first-rate outfit and it will reach its goal.

I beg you to greet all comrades for me; in my next dispatch I will write personally to several of them. Today it is not possible.

Nor has it been possible to keep Carlos Franqui and Eduardo up to date on everything as I had promised them. Now I am going to gather all I can about what is going on in the province and I will send it on to you. A big hug for everyone. Camilo.

During our march we took four Springfields in addition to the nine captured by Che.

Llanos de Santa Clara, October 9, 1958
(From *The Campaign Log of Comandante Camilo Cienfuegos*)

Chapter Ten

VILMA

I spoke on the telephone to Frank eight or ten minutes before he was killed. You know, he didn't even tell me that he was surrounded and that Salas Cañizares was there? Yes, the police were already there, but he said nothing, a normal everyday conversation.

Two days had gone by without Frank telephoning me. I called his place but nobody was there. It was strange, his disappearing like that, and I was worried. He was staying in a house which had always bothered me—the one where he was killed—because it had only one exit. We had rejected this house, but he was

175

so desperate after finding nothing else that he finally took it.

At last I got an answer when I phoned this time. He had already called me twice without getting anybody. "Why haven't you telephoned me? What's going on?" I asked. He said nothing of what was happening to him. He was in a hurry, I could sense that. Ten minutes after hanging up I heard gun shots in Santiago. I got back on the line to Frank's house and some stranger told me, "You've got the right place. I think there's a man on the roof and they're firing at him."

I learned of Frank's death in the most brutal fashion imaginable. I was notified by an operator from the telephone company, "There's a call being made by Salas Cañizares." You know that I was plugged in on all the enemy's communications. I heard all the calls made by Salas Cañizares, Río Chaviano and other Batista henchmen.

The operator notified me. Cañizares was telephoning his colleague Laureano Ibarra. And you know what I heard? "We got him, that filthy blankety-blank. Out there, we brought him down. Here's Basol." And Basol said, "Listen, chief," I think they had Tabernilla now on the line, "those three thousand pesos that you promised me, okay, I'm ready to collect." Three thousand pesos for having killed Frank!

Pujol had left his car at the corner of the street, a rented car, then he came around to the house and told Frank, "Come with me." Pujol behaved magnificently. They went out into the street slowly. But there was Randisch, the short Negro who had twice identified Frank. The police had brought him there for that purpose. Later on we executed him. Well, he pointed Frank out and they arrested him. Then Pujol's wife began screaming. They put the two boys in a car but, less than two hundred yards further, they made them get out to be killed.

We knew how Frank died because, although everybody was afraid and all shut their blinds, a little old lady remained at hers watching. She said that he lowered his head and they fired one shot in the back of his neck. He fell forward, arms outstretched. Pujol, too, was killed there.

Do you remember those signs, "Down with the Assassins!" in the 1953 demonstration? Because of the atrocities on Moncada? Well, Frank and his comrades were responsible for them. They said nothing, kept them hidden. Then the police came and said we couldn't attend the protest. They finally gave in. "All right, go—but on condition you do nothing against the Armed Forces." We told them we'd do nothing like that, but as soon as we paraded out of the school building, we unfurled the signs. The demonstration didn't last more than a few hundred yards, but we had accomplished what we set out to do, right in front of their water hoses.

I remember that when they began hosing they put one knee on the ground and aimed low. Everybody scattered and I hid under a porch. But you know Nilsa, she stayed put in the middle of the street and said, "Look, they're shooting at us!" I had to grab her and pull her away.

We went down the street and police cars came, picked up the young people and drove away. When we reached the market, fearing they would seize our photo equipment, we hid it in a banana crate and left it there. They started rounding up even younger people. I think Frank was there. They handcuffed them and got ready to lead them on foot because there were no more cars. They lined them up like a chain gang.

Then the butchers of the market interceded brandishing their work tools and said they wouldn't let them take anybody away. So the police let the kids go because—well, you've seen those butcher knives haven't you?

There was one incident—a small fellow resisted arrest, and the cop stuck the barrel of his revolver in his stomach. Well, the fellow slapped the cop, with that revolver against his stomach and all!

Many things like that happened. It was like a movie.

The day after the attack on Moncada there was more shooting. Maybe they were killing our comrades, I thought.

I said, "I'm going to see what's going on," and Ansela said she'd come along. We met two women from Bayamo we'd never seen before. They said, "Oh God, we're going there too!" They got into a bus right ahead of us.

Then we reached San Félix y Enramada. You know the population over there—the police are afraid of them! People were in the middle of the street, talking angrily, because they knew what was going on without knowing exactly who was being killed. You could hear gun shots and could tell they were killing people. All the time, trucks were carrying bodies to the cemetery. There was a terrible anger in those streets.

A policeman in a jeep was reading a newspaper but he really wasn't reading anything at all. He was hiding behind his paper and glancing right and left. He was scared! The people were indignant.

It was that indignation of the 26th of July, that desperate will to save the prisoners, which created the conditions for what happened later. Because of that, people became so opposed to such a massacre being repeated on the 30th of November of '56.

You know, every time Yeyé passes by behind the hospital she says it pains her because she believes that if they had gone that way after the attack, those now dead would have been able to save themselves. But they didn't think of it. Well, afterwards came the experiences of the 30th when our rebel comrades ran to take cover in homes and the people in them burned their uniforms for them and hid their arms, without even knowing who the rebels were. . . . Once I saved myself by crossing over a rooftop to another house. And do you know? Nobody said anything? The whole neighborhood was in on our conspiracy.

We stayed there after November 30. In January there was a wide search in the city and our house served all purposes; as a meeting place, a storehouse, an arsenal; anyone leaving for the Sierra was briefed there; it was a contact point until the next April.

There were problems; the police had informers in the neighborhood. We knew it, but we stayed there because in the beginning it was difficult to find a house. And, despite everything, we could do what we had to do, thanks to our neighbors who would tell us, "Now the stool-pigeon's going to such and such place." From a little farther on we'd get word again, "Now he's going in for coffee. Take advantage of it." Everybody was on the team.

Sometimes people would warn, "Things are stirring, they say there's going to be a search," and we would send all our boys on to another house in the neighborhood.

I met Raul in Mexico during two nerve-wracking days. I had been in the U. S. A., and in June, 1956, I got to Mexico, before returning to Santiago to prepare for November 30.

From that moment on nothing else mattered except preparing for the *Granma's* landing. Fidel asked for maps and other documents. I went to discuss the matter with Frank.

Frank left around September to arrange the final details. He went to Mexico twice.

Yes, it was in Mexico that I met Raul for the first time. We never dreamed that later on we would get married! I remember telling him that he had cheated me, because Fidel said, "Okay, tomorrow you'll get some training in the field," and then Raul called to say there wasn't any ammunition for me. Later, when I reminded him about "being cheated" he replied it wasn't so, it had been Sunday and Sundays we didn't

have training because there were too many strangers
around.

Then I saw him again up in the Sierra when Matthews came. But there still wasn't anything between
us. In fact, it was only after the opening of the Second
Front that we began going together.

You know, going into the Sierra was a relief for us.
When one of us was exhausted, he took a few days'
vacation in the Sierra. If there was a message to carry,
it was given to the one most in need of rest. They kept
telling me all the time, "The next message, you go,"
because I was already knocked out. But there was
always something to prevent me from going. I had
to wait a year, until February, 1958. Then I spent
a month and a half there.

I was in the Sierra Maestra on March 10. Raul came
one way, Almeida another and I came up a third.
After the meeting in which the general strike was decided upon, I returned to the city. After the strike I
wanted to go to the Second Front to find out whether
Raul would be coming to the new meeting that Fidel
had called and, also, to see whether he had something
to report back.

Another thing I wanted to discuss with Raul was
the rebel group that had been formed in the course of
the strike. Those strikers who had been activists before
and now found themselves exposed were going to
get together and rejoin the Second Front. Daniel had
been put in charge of this task but we had to recall
him because he was needed elsewhere. It was Aníbal
Castillo who remained with them. He was called

Comandante Aníbal. His group was expected to come through Filipinas. As it turned out, the same day I spoke to Raul about them the advancing men had attacked the barracks at Las Yaguas, put the enemy to flight and killed many of the guards.

Another time, we had decided to leave for the Sierra the next day so that we'd reach Manzanillo before nightfall. Early in the morning the others left, but Yeyé remained. She was going on the next-to-last trip that day while I would be on the last one so I'd have time to prepare some things for the Second Front, a few packages and some boots. In fact, when the Military Intelligence people came in, the wrapped-up boots were on the sofa—but they didn't see them. I was about to use the telephone and Yeyé was with me. I was in my bathrobe.

Over there people did not know Yeyé. She could pay Armando visits in prison. She acted as if she weren't mixed up in anything. When Military Intelligence arrived, she didn't budge. She was very tall and wore her hair short and was dressed like a peasant— you'd have sworn that she was a peasant. She always wore blouses and long skirts. Nobody ever recognized her. We always said she was the best one for disguises.

Yeyé told me, "Hurry up! There they are!" I grabbed a bag where I kept all our papers and ran to the back. There was a corridor to a terrace. The Intelligence men were already climbing the stairs and I leaped to the terrace. Yeyé was receiving them as I got out.

You know how people may do the unthinkable in

emergencies. I could never do again what I did that
day! The wall back there was made of bricks and I
went down it by the fingernails, the ends of my
fingers digging into the gaps between the bricks.
Without making a sound I got to the courtyard below.
I knew a large family lived there and that the lady
was the mother of the Armiñáns. I figured, "They have
a son in with the group so they won't say anything."
But I was afraid they'd scream and attract attention
from the outside. Can you picture it? I was in a bathrobe, hair disheveled, and climbing down from the
roof with a bag full of papers.

When I got down there, the women were hanging
laundry. One of them turned to me and stood still,
hands raised as if in prayer, staring at me. I had to
find something to say. You know what I said? "Hello,
am I in Doctor Armiñán's place?" Just as if I'd
knocked at the door! The woman screamed and fled,
followed by the others.

She later told me she had thought at that moment
I was the Holy Virgin who had suddenly appeared to
her. Soon after January first I met her again and she
explained, "I actually thought you were the Holy
Virgin. Then I looked you over and saw you were
wearing a bathrobe. I thought, the Virgin in a bathrobe?" The woman decided I had to be a lunatic
escaped from the asylum.

Finally they did figure out who I was because they
knew me by sight. I told the doctor's daughter to
phone him and say his mother was not feeling well.
She really did have heart trouble. When he arrived I

asked him to circle the block to see what was up. "Surrounded," he said. "You can't go out now."

I stayed there an hour. The police were searching everywhere upstairs, but they must have been looking only for a person, because they didn't go through any of our papers or packages. They looked in the closets and all the other places in which someone could hide.

I had to go climb up the same wall later and the women were dying of laughter. Ansela said, "Get a net for that messed-up hair so you can go out of the house!" I answered her, "Didn't have time to select one!" It was always like that. When something didn't end in violence it ended in laughter. . . .

Once in the house at Miramar del Pino in the Sierra, Yeyé, Celia and I were lying in a large bed. Imagine one of those little field-mice—well, I was half asleep but I felt something pulling at my hair. I jumped up, shrieking, "A mouse!" Celia, who lived in terror of mice, leaped out of bed and fell back, sitting on Yeyé. What a panic!

For the capture of Nicaro all the comandantes were mobilized. That was a formidable sight. When we got there a Chinese ship was in port and from the dock some of us greeted the crew. We went all over town. I went to the home of comrades who were engineers and I ate with some friends.

We settled in a hotel at Levisa. They opened fire early in the morning. I was just starting to brush my teeth. You know, bombings always caught me like that. I never got to finish brushing my teeth!

That time they were bombing us from frigates. How those shells from the frigates whistled overhead!

We were almost captured. The guards nearly caught us from the rear. Some of Sosa Blanco's men. We were in a house, evaluating incoming information and directing operations. We had left that hotel during the heavy bombing. All of a sudden we heard a barrage nearby. We ran out in the street and Raul told me to get in a jeep and take the radio with me. I drove with a comrade while scout planes wheeled above, machine-gunning us. And that was when the jeep chose to get stuck in the mud, at a spot that had no trees, nothing! You can imagine how hard I shoved that jeep with my shoulder! I tell you, when things are really rough, you do things that would normally be plain impossible.

It was Daniel who baptized me Deborah. After Frank's death. Before that I was Monica. Since Frank had my name in his notebook, the police came to my place. But I had left the night before. There was my telephone number with the name, Monica. They decided to change my name.

At that particular time all the comrades were getting names beginning with *D*. That's why I got to be Deborah.

Frank had been Salvador for a while, then David and finally, for a few days before his death, Christian.

Daniel was always Daniel. But at the start we referred to him as "the man from Nicaro."

The interview of Fidel and Raul by Cantillo took

place December 28. It had already been decided that Fidel would march on Palma and Efigenio would attack Guantánamo City. As to Raul, he was to set up near Santiago in preparation for the battle of Santiago.

One night Papa had come to ask us to dine with him Christmas Day. Then we had decided to stay at Ermita the 31st to welcome in the New Year. We went to sleep at midnight. Alcoholic drinks were forbidden on the Second Front so we had soft drinks.

At six in the morning the people we were staying with told me, "The radio says Batista's fled!" I woke up Raul and we decided to join Fidel. Raul spoke to Efigenio's men, who were leaving for Guantánamo. We retraced our steps to Palma to have a talk with Fidel, but we found him en route to the city.

They left for Santiago without me; they didn't want me to go with them. But what really burned me up was that when Fidel saw me later he asked, "Why didn't you go with the others?" If I'd known Fidel would say that I would have sneaked in among them. Because, after all, it's the Commander in Chief who does the deciding!

Finally, though, we all did get down to the city, and about one in the morning Fidel made a speech. What an uproar! Everybody had gotten up, everybody was in the streets, women in hairnets, men in pajamas. People were running out of houses crying and carrying almost all of us on their shoulders. The whole town had gathered in the park to listen to Fidel.

Fidel returned to Havana on the 8th and on the 20th he sent for us. Raul and I had already decided to get married on the 26th of December. . . .

APPENDIX

I: EVENTS

March 10, 1952: Colonel Batista's military coup overthrows constitutional government, establishing dictatorship. Students and youth organize demonstrations, repressed by force.

July 26, 1953: Fidel Castro, with 150 youths, attacks Moncada barracks at Santiago de Cuba. Attack fails but the insurrectionary movement is born of that defeat.

October 16, 1953: Fidel Castro, a prisoner, makes defense speech for revolutionary ideology of 26th of July Movement that instantly becomes rallying cry for opposition. (History Will Absolve Me.)

187

December 2, 1956: Castro leaves Mexico, where he took refuge
following amnesty, to lead expeditionary force of 82 men
on yacht *Granma*. They land at Belic, near Santiago,
while Frank País attacks with city irregulars inside Santiago.

December 5, 1956: Expedition survivors, tracked by army,
ambushed at Alegría del Pío; many captured or killed.

December 5-17, 1956: For 11 days, Castro, Universo Sánchez
and Faustino Pérez, live on sugar cane. They evade
Batista's soldiers.

December 18, 1956: 12 survivors of expedition (the Twelve)
regroup around Fidel Castro, organize first guerilla unit
in Sierra Maestra Mountains.

January 17, 1957: The Twelve, with 5 peasants who join them,
attack La Plata military post. Capture 10 weapons and
have first victory.

February 17, 1957: Herbert Matthews, *New York Times* news-
man, arrives in Sierra and announces guerilla's existence
to world.

March 13, 1957: Revolutionary Directorate, a student group,
attacks Presidential Palace, Batista's residence.

April-May, 1957: Havana without electricity 3 days following
rebels' sabotage. Terrorism spreads throughout country.

May 28, 1957: Sierra guerillas attack El Uvero, important
military post, seize large ammunition stores.

July 30, 1957: Police arrest Frank País, underground leader
of 26th of July Movement and kill him at Santiago.
Funeral crowds of women fired on by police. General
strike for 3 days at Santiago.

September 5, 1957: City of Cienfuegos briefly seized by Rebel
groups.

November, 1957: First free territory organized at El Hombrito
in Sierra. Tactical warfare begins.

March, 1958: Night of 100 bombs in Havana.
Raul Castro leads column from Sierra, opens Second
Front in mountains of north.
Camilo Cienfuegos, with another column, descends to
plains at Bayamo and attacks army.

Juan Almeida, with third column, attacks army at El Cobre, near Santiago.

April 9, 1958: National strike fails due to timing errors and lack of popular support. Serious setback for insurrection.

May, 1958: Batista mobilizes all military resources, launches 14 battalions, backed by planes, artillery and marines, in vast offensive against Sierra Maestra guerillas.

June, 1958: Capture and later release of Americans aiding Batista.

June 28, 1958: Army seizes 90% of Rebel territory. 300 poorly-armed guerillas, short of ammunition, resist 2,000 soldiers.

June 29, 1958: Rebel column inflicts serious defeat on army, captures many prisoners and large stores, at Santo Domingo in Sierra Maestra.

July, 1958: 250 soldiers killed or captured in 11 days of combat at El Jigüe. Few days later prisoners turned over to International Red Cross.

August 7, 1958: Army driven from all Sierra Maestra.

August 18, 1958: 6 columns of 100 men each, armed with weapons taken from army, spread across Cuba. Growing demoralization of Batista forces.

November 3, 1958: Popular repudiation of Batista-rigged elections. Mass executions fail to halt attacks and sabotage.

November-December, 1958: Camilo Cienfuegos' column crosses 3 provinces to reach northern part of central Cuba. Che Guevara's column, in south, reaches Escambray Mountains, linking up with other guerillas. Fidel Castro, Raul Castro and Juan Almeida, having liberated most of Oriente Province, advance on Santiago with their columns.

December 29, 1958: Che Guevara takes city of Santa Clara. Seizes munitions train, over 1,000 prisoners taken by the Rebels.

December 31, 1958: Batista flees to the Dominican Republic.

January 1, 1959: Fidel Castro appeals for general strike, orders all columns to march on Havana and other cities. Strike total success. Santiago surrenders.

January 8, 1959: Fidel Castro arrives in Havana, makes important political statements, announces dismissal and departure of U.S. military mission.

II: PLACES

Sierra Maestra: La Plata, El Turquino Peak, El Uvero, Jigüe, Las Mercedes, Vegas de Jibacoa, El Macho, El Ají de Juana, El Lomón, El Infierno, Caguara.

Other places in Oriente Province: Santiago de Cuba, Moncada, San Félix de Enramada, Boniato, Siboney, Celda, Alegría del Pío, Belic, Pilón, Niquero, Manzanillo, Bayamo, El Cobre, Yateras, Guantánamo, Nicaro.

Province of Havana: Prison of the Isle of Pines, Artemisa, Prado 109, University Hill, Virgen del Camino.

Other places: Vuelta Abajo, Pinar del Río, Goicuría, Matanzas, Camagüey, Las Villas, Yaguajay, Trocha de Júcaro a Morón.

III: BATISTA'S AGENTS AND POLICE

Tabernilla, Salas Cañizares, Masferrer, Cowley, Pilar García, Ventura, Faget, Piedra, Frometa, Basol, Ponce, Chicho Osorio, Matico, Manolo Capitan, Río Chaviano, Chaumont, Casillas, Laureano Ibarra, Ruiz.